Along and Around the
Greensand Way
Haslemere - Westerham - Hamstreet

ACKNOWLEDGEMENTS

We are grateful to the following bodies and individuals for their assistance in route development and in preparation of this guidebook:

Centre for Kentish Studies, Maidstone
Church Histories
Country Houses
District and Borough Councils
English Nature – Kent Team
English Nature – Surrey and Sussex Team
Environment Agency
Farmers
Forest Enterprises
Kent County Council Highways and Transportation Department
Kent Wildlife Trust
Landowners for personal comment
Local libraries
Local museums
Parish Councils
Surrey Local Studies Library, Guildford
Surrey Wildlife Trust
The National Trust
Woodland Trust

The development, interpretation and promotion of the Greensand Way in Kent has been achieved with financial assistance from the Countryside Commission.

COUNTRYSIDE COMMISSION

Guidebooks in this series also available:

Eden Valley Walk
Elham Valley Way
Darent Valley Path
High Weald Walk
Medway Valley Walk
Stour Valley Walk

Other route guidebooks are planned and in preparation. .

Copies of these guidebooks can be obtained from bookshops, tourist information centres, libraries and post free from the Access and Recreation Officer, Kent County Council, Planning Department, Springfield, Maidstone Kent ME14 2LX.

Surrey County Council publish packs of circular walks and stock other publications. For a complete list, write to Marketing and Communications, Environment, Surrey County Council, County Hall, Kingston-upon-Thames, Surrey KT1 2DY.

Along and Around the
Greensand Way
Haslemere - Westerham - Hamstreet

Produced by the Rights of Way Group, Surrey County Council and Countryside Group, Kent County Council.

Designed by The Bubblegate Company Ltd, 40 Broad Street, Canterbury, Kent CT1 2LR.

Author – Bea Cowan, Illustrator – Matthew Cook, Photographers – Bea Cowan, Tim Fagan
and Surrey County Council.

Maps produced by Ordnance Survey following a style developed by The Design Studio, Kent County Council.
Reproduced from the Ordnance Survey Pathfinder maps with the permission of the
Controller of Her Majesty's Stationery Office © Crown copyright.
Unauthorised reproduction infringes Crown copyright and may lead to prosecution or civil proceedings.
LA 076708/97/05.
Ordnance Survey and Pathfinder are registered trade marks and the OS symbol a trademark of
Ordnance Survey, the National Mapping Agency of Great Britain.

Printed in Great Britain by Heanorgate Printing Ltd, Heanor, Derbyshire DE75 7SJ

Published jointly by Environment, Surrey County Council, County Hall, Kingston upon Thames, Surrey KT1 2DY, and
Kent Environment & Planning Agency, Kent County Council, Springfield, Maidstone, Kent ME14 2LX
in association with Ordnance Survey.

First editions - 1989 Greensand Way in Surrey
1992 Greensand Way in Kent

Second edition – (updated and expanded – Surrey and Kent) October 1997.

ISBN   1 899706 35 6 Surrey County Council
1 873010 91 5 Kent County Council

CONTENTS

To the best of our knowledge, the interpretative content and all other information is believed to be correct. We should be grateful if you would inform us of any changes, omissions or errors, so that modifications can be made in revisions of the book.

Greensand Ridge

INTRODUCTION

The Greensand Way takes the walker along paths which in many places give unparalleled views across the Weald to the south. At many places there are extensive views towards the North Downs. Frequently, the route leads through quiet, almost remote areas. Much of the land is designated an area of Outstanding Natural Beauty (AONB); the stretch from Hindhead to Leith Hill has formed part of the Surrey Hills AONB since 1958. The Sevenoaks ridge, from the Surrey-Kent border to Borough Green, is included in the Kent Downs AONB.

Geology

The Greensand ridge consists of a series of layers of sandstone in each of which the green-coloured mineral, glauconite, is found in varying degrees. As the glauconite is exposed to the atmosphere, it oxidises and acquires the yellow, somewhat mud-coloured, tinge found in the rough stones you see along much of the Way. The building stone of the Upper Greensand sometimes may have a greenish tinge when wet due to the high iron oxide content.

The Greensand was first formed in Lower Cretaceous times around 120 million years ago. At this time the last of the Jurassic rocks had long been formed and the Wealden clays and sandstones of the Lower Cretaceous period, seen today in the High Weald, deposited above them. The weight of these sandstones caused the area to subside and sea entered.

The Areas of Outstanding Natural Beauty

Orchard and converted oast houses at Barn Hill

For around 10 million years sedimentary, marine deposits were laid down and grains of sand were cemented together by silica to form sandstones. These deposits created the different formations of the Lower Greensand - Atherfield Clay, Hythe Beds, Sandgate Beds and Folkestone Beds.

During the next 10 million years the sea gradually became deeper and further deposits were laid down, first of Gault Clay, then of the Upper Greensand layers of a loose sandstone, compacted in different degrees, and sometimes known as malmstone. Subsequent deposits above the strata of the Greensand formed the chalk.

Around 100 million years ago extensive earth movements, probably connected with those which formed the Alps, pushed the centre of the Weald upwards to form a dome, uplifting and folding the different layers. Weathering and erosion by wind, rain and the deep frosts of the Ice Ages removed younger or softer rocks from the surface. In the centre remained the sands and clays of the High Weald, surrounded by Wealden clay. Further out rose the Greensand ridge, then the Downs, their

Geological map of south-east England

scarp faces the result of the fierce movements that uplifted them.

The Greensand emerged as a horseshoe-shaped ridge. The Hythe Beds form the escarpment. Erosion by wind and rain, landslips on the steep scarp face, and solifluction (a mass of earth moving over frozen ground) have further combined to create steep-sided combes, and low hillocks below the scarp. Today the scarp rises steeply in the west between Gibbet Hill and its highest point Leith Hill (967 feet). The scarp flattens for several miles, then re-emerges east of Nutfield and runs eastward, with a break at the Medway gap, as far as Pluckley. From there on the land levels until it drops at the old cliff line above the Romney Marsh.

The sandstones have all been extensively quarried over many centuries. To the west in Surrey the Sandgate Beds and Bargate Beds, which lie above the Hythe Beds, have yielded the distinctive yellow stone seen in many buildings of this region. Ironstone, from layers embedded in the Sandgate Beds, is often seen in the chips pressed into the mortar between such stones. To the east, especially in the area round Maidstone, the Hythe Beds yield a blue-grey sandstone with a high lime content. Known as ragstone, this is seen in many old buildings along the Way in Kent. Fuller's earth which lies interbedded between the Bargate and Sandgate layers has been much quarried where it occurs near Reigate and near Maidstone.

The Folkestone Beds consist of seams of pebbles and sand. It is from here that the stone known as Chert is found, familiar in the Chart Hills around Limpsfield. The word comes from the Scandinavian Kartr meaning stony ground. You may see areas between Dorking and Redhill where the more sandy parts of the formation have been excavated. Above the Gault Clay, the Upper Greensand yields a sandstone with a

strong silica content. Due to the incline of the dip slope this lies further north, running at an angle downwards beneath the North Downs. Between Brockham and Reigate, malmstone was formerly quarried for building stone. One variety, firestone, was used to line furnaces; a second variety, hearthstone, for whitening hearths.

Landscape

Many factors have combined to shape the Greensand landscape we see today. A crucial element was the growth of the woodland cover throughout the country. From around 8,000 BC, birch and willow spread northwards from Europe, followed by Scots pine, hazel, oak and elm. This resulted, in the South East, in the great forest known as Andredsweal (the wood behind Anderida, the Roman name for Pevensey), which covered the entire Wealden area. Once the English Channel had separated Britain from the Continent, around 4,000 BC, few species arrived. The landscape then developed through a close interaction between people and their environment as the trees were felled for timber and to

provide grazing and arable land or as sand and stone were extracted from the ground. Heathland developed in Neolithic times on sandy soil where clearance and grazing depleted the soil.

By the 17th century the Weald had lost most of its original woodland cover. The few new stretches of ancient semi-natural woodland which still survive, that is woodland over 400 years

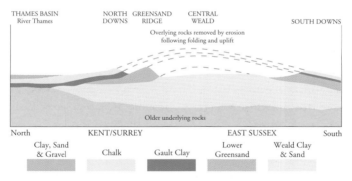

Outline geological section across the Downs and Weald

THAMES BASIN
River Thames

NORTH DOWNS

GREENSAND RIDGE

CENTRAL WEALD

SOUTH DOWNS

Overlying rocks removed by erosion following folding and uplift

Older underlying rocks

North   KENT/SURREY   EAST SUSSEX   South

Clay, Sand & Gravel   Chalk   Gault Clay   Lower Greensand   Weald Clay & Sand

old, are carefully conserved. In other areas secondary woodland has grown up, and beech and birch are dominant. Coppicing has been practised over many centuries where trees are cut to near-ground level and allowed to regrow over a period of years. Parkland and gardens often created in the 17th

century have left their mark. In Surrey some pine woods also date from this time.

Industry

For many centuries, in both Surrey and Kent, sheep-rearing provided a staple industry. In medieval and Tudor times many small villages and towns flourished as a result, with cloth-making and fulling round Maidstone and Witley. Surrey

in particular became an important manufacturing county, dependent on its natural resources: to make glass at Cranleigh and near Hambledon, iron near Haslemere. By the 16th and 17th centuries many of its rivers to the north, including the Tillingbourne and the Mole, provided water power

to work mills for iron, brass, cloth, paper and gunpowder. Quarrying and mining dominated the Upper Greensand area below the North Downs. After the Industrial Revolution moved the country's centre of industry northwards, Surrey's villages lost considerable income.

Agriculture and horticulture

The Greensand soils have given rise to a varied pattern in agriculture. In Kent the Hythe Beds produced a relatively rich and loamy soil well suited to crops and fruit, while the heavier Sandgate Beds yield good, moist pasture. Farmed to some degree from early times, from the 16th century on, these lands saw considerable increase in production. In Surrey the poor, sandy soil of the Greensand ridge provided ample grazing for cattle and pigs, while the Upper Greensand of the clay valley, the Vale of Holmsdale, yielded better crops. The 19th century saw an expansion of cereal production. In recent years there has been a sharp decrease in this, whereas production of maize, oilseed rape and linseed has increased.

continued on page 11

The design of the Greensand Way logo in Kent is based on the oast house which, with its distinctive cowl, is a traditional feature of the Kent countryside. (In Surrey, the letters GW appear inside the waymark arrow.)

These buildings were used to dry hops in readiness for beer-making. The word oast is so named from the old English word for drying. In the early days of hop growing, the fruit, known as the 'cone', was dried in the sun. This method was clearly unreliable and farmers started to dry their hops in standard barns. Then, once the hop industry had become established and the outlay was considered worthwhile, farmers developed a system of drying indoors.

The design of the oast house, originally rectangular, and looking much like the standard barn, was introduced from Holland in the 17th century. The building contained three rooms, one for loading, one for drying, one for cooling.

Square oast houses followed, then, in the early 19th century, round, as drying techniques changed. Finally the square form returned to favour. The cowl, traditionally made by a wheelwright, evolved at the end of the 18th century. It formed a crucial part of the structure, being designed to create a vacuum which would draw the hot air through the oast house. The characteristic wind vane, extending from the cowl, was a 19th-century addition. The position of the vane varies from oast to oast. In mid Kent you will find it near the base of the cowl. In east Kent, where the vane is far shorter, you will find it at the top. The vane was frequently embellished with a finial, often with a motif, the favourite motif in Kent being the rampant horse.

Today many hedges have long since been removed and, instead of the traditional patchwork of smaller fields, you will see large fields of around 400 acres, required to make a living. On smaller farms pasture and grazing now predominate and sheep rearing is seeing an increase. You will also see fields set aside from production, in accordance with European policy.

Orchards have by tradition flourished on the Greensand, especially on the free-draining loam of the Hythe Beds in Kent. Production of top-fruit (apples, pears, etc) has declined in recent years in Surrey but Kent remains a major fruit-producing area, recalling its title the 'Garden of England'. Today you will seldom see the traditional orchard, with 'standard' fruit trees. Instead you can see closely packed 'bush' varieties on dwarfing root stock. Many orchards shown even on recent maps have been grubbed out and replanted.

Hops were first introduced into Kent from Flanders at the end of the 15th century. At first many people opposed the use of hops in beer, considering them 'an unwholesome weed' which

adulterated good ale. By the 16th century hop growing played an established part in farming throughout much of Kent and Sussex and in the west of Surrey in the Farnham area. Hop growing reached its peak in England in the 19th century. Although the industry has declined since the early part of this century, as the result of overseas competition, research has continued and production may now be increasing again. Many oast houses, where hops were dried, have now been converted but you will still see the distinctive cowl with its weather-vane in many parts of Kent.

Natural history

The sandstones of the Greensand ridge vary from acidic to calcareous and provide a variety of wildlife habitats. The sandy soils to the west in Surrey on the Hythe Beds are acidic. Where there is open heathland you will find the dominant ling heather (Calluna vulgaris) with patches of bell heather (Erica cinerea). Here there is usually a good invert-ebrate population. Heathland also occurs on outcrops of the Folkestone Beds at Reigate Heath and Hothfield Common.

Where grazing has ceased, one-time heathland has often been invaded by acid-loving secondary woodland with trees such as birch, pedunculate oak and Scots pine. Areas of extreme acidity still support the ling heather. Beneath the trees a rich ground flora may develop,

Fish at Chartwell

with bluebells, wood sage and wood sorrel. These woodlands, as well as the rare stretches of ancient semi-natural woodland, such as Leith Hill Place Woods are ideal habitats for a wide range of birds.

Between Nutfield and Godstone old quarries and sand pits are now filled with water. Along with the open agricultural land they attract many birds. At Godstone interesting habitats occur where chalk streams flow

over the sandstone and enable plant communities which support specific invertebrates and breeding birds to thrive.

The areas of land now owned by the National Trust around Toys Hill and Ide Hill, largely designated Sites of Special

Scientific Interest (SSSI), show well the sequence of plant communities as you descend the slopes over the different Greensand strata. Here you will see beech, sessile and pedunculate oak on the acidic plateau with birch, whitebeam and rowan. Lower down pedunculate oak predominates, with bramble, wood sorrel and honeysuckle in the ground flora. Next, where lime is present in the soil you find field maple, wild cherry and hazel in the canopy, while on the wet, alkaline soil of the local Wealden clay you find guelder rose in the canopy and bugle, dog's mercury and wood-sedge in the undergrowth. Woodland management has always created diverse habitats, as the mixture of coppice with standards, carefully managed at Ham Street Woods, today reveals.

History and archaeology

The geology and landscape of the South East have greatly affected the pattern of settlement throughout the region. Inevitably Kent was the first of the two areas to be settled, as successive groups of people crossed the land bridge which joined Britain and the Continent. Worked flints found near Limpsfield give some signs of early man in this area but not until around 10,000 BC did Palaeolithic people venture further south as revealed by the many microliths, very small flints worked into blades and tools, found, in particular, on the heathland of south-west Surrey. From around 6,000 BC Middle Stone Age people began to clear the forests and graze the sandy slopes. Farming was more widely introduced by Neolithic

Flints and ashlar, Holy Trinity Church, Westcott

farmers from around 4,000 BC. Haslemere was settled from around 2,500 BC. Sites have also been found at Leith Hill, Wotton, Reigate and Redhill, also near Ightham, and at Roughway.

Around 2,000 BC new settlers brought the ability and skill to work in bronze and introduced new pottery. Their most striking remains are the bowl or barrow mounds, their burial sites, such as those found, beside the Glory Wood near Dorking, on Reigate Heath, and near Egerton.

From around the fifth and fourth centuries BC Celtic people began to arrive. They introduced the use of iron and developed agriculture throughout the South East. Threatened by the Belgae from about the second century BC they occupied many of the southern outcrops of the ridge, such as Hascombe Hill, Pitch Hill, Holmbury Hill and Anstiebury Hill. This series of hill forts has yielded evidence of 'shot' for sling warfare, and in places has shown signs of rapid

evacuation. They may well have been centres of defence, established to protect farming communities further north, or to guard their interests in the iron available in the Weald. In Kent, strong earthwork ramparts were established at Squerryes Camp above Westerham and at Oldbury, north of Ightham.

After the Claudian invasion of AD43 the Romans established links for defence and trade. From then on all main roads centred on London which became the hub of the South East. In Kent two roads, one to Hastings, the other to Lympne, met just west of Sutton Valence. On the Kent/Surrey border the London to Lewes Way ran up the ridge near Limpsfield Chart. In Surrey, Stane Street ran from Chichester to London over the Holmwood and through Dorking. The London to Brighton Way ran near Godstone over Tilburstow Hill. Other, smaller roads linked with these. In Kent small Roman settlements occur along the ridge, as at Little Chart, Chart Sutton and Boughton Monchelsea. A cemetery lay near the road at Sutton Valence. In Surrey a temple stood at Farley Heath, reached by a branch road from Stane Street.

The Saxon period continued the pattern of scattered settlements, again with more known in Kent than in Surrey. Augustine re-introduced Christianity to England in 597 and, soon after, abbeys were founded in Canterbury and at Chertsey. The spread of Christianity may have been helped by the unification under the one kingdom of Mercia of both 'Sudergeona', the 'southern region', and Kent, which derives its name from the Celtic tribe Cantiaci.

Well-defined communities developed, based on the parish and the manor. In Kent a line of churches was established along the ridge. In Surrey, Witley influenced a wide area while Tandridge, further east, was at the centre of its administrative division, the 'Hundred'. In later medieval times new parishes were created and land was parcelled out as more manors, such as Ightham, were created. Some manors and their houses declined but others such as Knole and Godinton increased in size and dignity. In Kent the law of Gavelkind held, rather than the law of primogeniture. Each son inherited equally so land was frequently subdivided into smaller holdings.

Communications were enhanced as roads improved and canals were built. The turnpike system devised in the 18th century further helped by introducing tolls which transferred the cost of road maintenance from local inhabitants to the road users.

Architecture

The architecture of Surrey and Kent has remarkable similarities as well as notable differences. Inevitably the stone of each locality provides a specific characteristic as you see in the stone used for the more prestigious buildings, firestone for Reigate Castle, ragstone for Sutton Castle. Churches too reflect their region, with Bargate stone in west Surrey, hearthstone at Brockham and ragstone nearly always used in Kent. Imported stone, whether from nearby Bethersden or more distant Portland, reflected a desire for ostentation or innovation.

In medieval times a central, open hearth was the norm in all houses. Peasants lived in small cottages of thin timber and daub, usually with only one room. In wealthier households in the South East the Wealden hall house evolved where a central hall provided the main living area, while a service area lay at one end, separated by a screen passage. Even larger houses had a private wing at the other end, often with accommodation above. Along the route lie many examples of such houses, which

remained timber framed until the 16th century.

Kent clays and brick-earth produced superb bricks and tiles in rich blues and reds. As bricks and tiles became cheaper those who could afford it installed chimneys and enclosed their houses, with hung tiles above and brick, inserted as understorey below. 'Mathematical' tiles were developed, flanged and made to look like bricks. Variations in design included methods of laying bricks - English and Flemish bonds. Weatherboarding provided an alternative cover. From the 16th century onwards, when Flemish Huguenots settled in east Kent, Dutch or shaped gables became popular with the gentry and upper classes. The 19th century saw a revival in vernacular architecture as Norman Shaw and others, notably, Edwin Lutyens, incorporated old styles in their designs for Victorian and Edwardian buildings.

Tennyson Memorial Window by E. Burne Jones, St Bartholomew's Church, Haslemere

Greensand Way

Walking advice

No season of the year is closed to walkers; enjoyment can be gained from walking on a bright crisp winter's morning or on an Indian Summer's day in the autumn. Equally rewarding is a springtime walk when the countryside is full of new life and growth.

Always wear suitable clothing and footwear for the season. Be prepared for changeable weather.

Take clothes which are warm and waterproof. Inexpensive overtrousers will give protection from any discomfort caused by walking through high vegetation or rain-drenched crops. Sections of paths may be muddy after periods of rain so wear strong, comfortable and waterproof footwear.

Allow plenty of time to complete your chosen walk. Reckon on walking 2 or 2½ miles an hour. The distances and times for each section of the walk are shown on the route maps, and in the information. Allow more time if it has been wet, if you are elderly, or have children or inexperienced walkers with you.

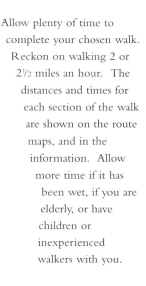

Country Code

Enjoy the countryside and respect its life and work.

Guard against all risk of fire.

Leave all gates as found.

Keep your dogs under close control.

Keep to public paths across farmland.

Use gates and stiles to negotiate fences, hedges and walls.

Leave livestock, crops and machinery alone.

Take your litter home.

Help to keep all water clean.

Protect wildlife, plants and trees.

Take special care on country roads.

Make no unnecessary noise.

The route has been established in consultation with landowners and farmers and follows public rights of way and permissive paths. Remember that most public paths cross private estates and farmland. Some evolved as routes from farms to the nearest village and were not designed for large numbers of people. Often you are walking through a place of work; enjoy the countryside but please have regard for its life and work. Crops and animals are the farmers' livelihood and should be left undisturbed.

Always keep to the path to avoid trespass and walk in single file through a crop. Report any obstructions or other problems to the appropriate Highway Authority, Surrey or Kent County Council (see page 19)

Take care when crossing or walking along country roads. Keep to the right, in single file, facing oncoming traffic. On a bend, however, walk on the outside and keep a good lookout for traffic.

Remember to leave things as found - refasten gates you find closed. Straying stock can cause damage and an expensive

A ploughman's lunch

inconvenience to farmers. Always use gates and stiles to negotiate fences and hedges.

Take your litter home - it can injure people, animals and wildlife. Guard against all risk of fire, especially in dry weather. Picnicking is not permitted on private land; you only have a right of passage on a right of way.

To avoid injury or distress to farm animals and wildlife, keep dogs under control at all times. If not on a lead they can run surprisingly long distances and consequently may be out of sight and the control of the owner. Please keep dogs on leads, particularly when passing through fruit growing areas, fields with standing crops or livestock, and heathland and woodlands. Farmers have a right to shoot dogs found worrying their livestock.

Using the guidebook

This book is designed to be a practical guide to walking the Greensand Way in either direction. It is a guidebook containing a route guide. It may be used intact or separately by carefully removing the weather-resistant route guide from the centre of the book. The guidebook contains a route description, specialist and other information and guidance on planning and preparing for a walk. The route guide, with route directions and information about features passed en route, is self-contained and can be

Thistledown

used independently of the guidebook.

The route maps have been arranged in sequence from Haslemere to Hamstreet. When walking from west to east, the book is used in a conventional way, whilst the east to west route is read from the back of the book to the front.

By carefully folding it back, the book and/or route guide will fit into a map case, thus providing protection against damage, dirt and damp.

Care should be taken when using the route directions since the countryside is constantly changing, with stiles, gates and field boundaries being removed or new ones erected. Route finding should not be a problem given the large scale route maps and the extensive waymarking and signing on the ground.

Route options

The Greensand Way is 108 miles long and can be undertaken as a long distance walk in about a week.

The walk can be undertaken in sections or shorter walks can be

continued on page 18

These pages are sponsored by Ordnance Survey

Maps

Ordnance Survey sheet numbers and titles:

LANDRANGER SERIES, scale 1:50,000 – 1¼ inches to 1 mile (2 cm to 1 km) These all-purpose maps include selected tourist information, caravan and camping sites, picnic areas and viewpoints and rights of way.

186	*Aldershot & Guildford*
187	*Dorking, Reigate & Crawley*
188	*Maidstone & The Weald of Kent*
189	*Ashford & Romney Marsh*

EXPLORER SERIES, scale 1:25,000 – 2½ inches to 1 mile (4cm to 1 km) These maps are the replacements for the Pathfinder Series which is being phased out. With larger area coverage, these highly detailed maps clearly depict the rights of way network as well as showing selected tourist information. The perfect walking companion, they are ideal if you want to devise your own walks in the area.

| 133 | *Haslemere & Petersfield* |
| 134 | *Crawley & Horsham* |

145	*Guildford & Farnham*
146	*Dorking & Leatherhead*
147	*Sevenoaks & Tonbridge*
148	*Maidstone & the Medway Towns*
136	*The Weald & Royal Tonbridge Wells*
137	*Ashford*
125	*Romney Marsh, Rye & Winchelsea*

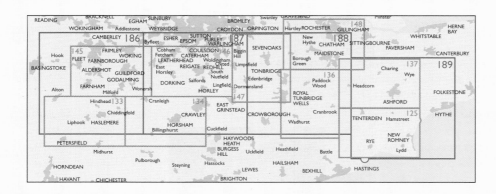

Pathfinder Guides

If you enjoyed the Greensand Way and wish to explore further the countryside of Surrey and Kent, OS/Jarrold Pathfinder Guides are ideal. The Pathfinder Guides to Kent and Surrey and Sussex provide further walking opportunities. Each includes 28 specially designed walks accompanied with clear, detailed 1:25,000 OS mapping. There are a range of walks from short, easy ones to more challenging expeditions and each one is colour coded to identify levels of difficulty. A useful cross-reference chart is featured further summarising the walks, including information on distances, time and start points, so you can pick out the walk to suit your preference and ability. With additional information on where to obtain refreshments, safety issues to be aware of when walking and scenic photographs, these books are the ideal walking companion.

Cycle Tours

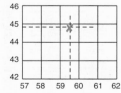

The Greensand Way is a promoted route for walkers only. However as an alternative to exploring the area on foot, you can take to your bike and enjoy a cycling exploration of Kent and Surrey. OS/Hamlyn Cycle Tours to Kent, Surrey and Sussex is the ideal accompaniment, detailing 14 on-road and 10 off-road routes. The tours are suitable for day rides, touring and mountain biking, and distances range from about 30-35 miles for on-road routes and 15-20 miles for off-road. Each route has clear and detailed instructions combined with Ordnance Survey 1:50,000 Landranger map extracts with the route clearly marked. All routes detail distance, the terrain you will encounter, tips for touring and an introduction on main features of the ride. Additional information is supplied on where to obtain refreshments, and places of interest to stop and see on route. Whether you wish to traverse pleasant countryside or villages, or tackle more challenging rides across the Downs, these well planned trips will have something to suit your mood.

To obtain the most up-to-date information on the maps available and for further information on Ordnance Survey maps and guides contact: Customer Information, Ordnance Survey, Romsey Road, Southampton, SO16 4GU, telephone (0345) 33 00 11.

Ordnance Survey maps covering the Greensand Way are available from bookshops, local tourist information centres and post free from Kent County Council, Planning Dept, Springfield, Maidstone, Kent ME14 2LX.

Grid References

The grid references of the starting and finishing points of each section of the route of the Greensand Way are given in the route guide.

The framework of squares spaced at one kilometre intervals over Ordnance Survey maps is known as the National Grid. The grid facilitates the pinpointing of any place in the country, giving it a unique reference number.

To give a reference number, first take the western (left-hand) edge of the kilometre square in which the place lies. Read the figures at the end of the line in the top and bottom margins of the map, then moving eastwards (to the right) estimate the position of the place in tenths across the square.

Secondly, take the southern edge of the map square and read the figures at the end of the line in the side margins of the map. Then, moving northwards, estimate the position of the place in tenths up the square. This gives the place a six figure reference number accurate to within 100 metres.

The grid reference of ✗ is at 595448

In finding out a grid reference, the first three numbers of the six figure number refer to the line and number of tenths across the square, whilst the second three numbers refer to the line and number of tenths up the square.

To provide more flexibility in route planning, the following Greensand Way link routes have been established:

In Surrey, to the North Downs Way from Westcott, Skimmington, and Oxted (follow the route maps and standard right of way waymarks).

In Kent, to Westerham, Sevenoaks, Charing and Ashford (follow the route maps and the Greensand Way link path waymarks).

devised, of a day or half-day's duration, depending on your ability and time availability, using the bus and train routes which link with many of the places along the route (look for the bus and rail symbols on the route maps).

If you wish to undertake the Greensand Way in sections or as a series of short walks you need to be aware of problems of returning to your starting point. Possible solutions might be as follows:
a) Using two cars, one at the starting point and the other at the proposed finishing point.
b) Using one car and public transport. If relying on infrequent bus services it is suggested that you make your outward journey by bus thus returning confidently to your car or base.
c) Retracing your steps - the scenery can look surprisingly different when walking in the opposite direction.

Waymarking and signing

The term waymarking refers to marking objects along a public right of way. It complements signposting, which shows where a right of way leaves the metalled road and indicates its initial direction, and enables users to follow a path accurately and confidently at points where they might otherwise have difficulty.

Waymarking benefits not only users of rights of way but also farmers and landowners. It increases users' enjoyment of the countryside and helps to prevent unintentional trespass.

Waymarking system
The recommended system in England and Wales uses small coloured arrows to show the direction of the path and also to act as a target when viewed from a distance. A different colour is used for each category of right of way, *see right:*

If the status of a path changes along its length, so does the colour of the waymarking arrows. Where a right of way is part of a special route, such as a National Trail, Recreation Route or Circular Walk, the arrows are used in conjunction with the route's own symbol.

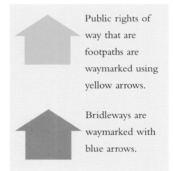

Public rights of way that are footpaths are waymarked using yellow arrows.

Bridleways are waymarked with blue arrows.

Byways open to all traffic and other routes that may legally be used by wheeled vehicles are waymarked with red arrows, but they are intended only to show the status of the route and not indicate whether it is physically suitable for vehicles.

Transport

Car parking
Places to park are shown on the route maps. Please note that these are not necessarily car parks. If a car park is not available, please park thoughtfully and sensibly to avoid causing an obstruction or damage to the roadside verges. Leave your car securely locked with valuables out of sight.

Walkers near Hamptons

Bus and train services

It is not practical to give details of all the bus and train routes and services to and along the Greensand Way, since they may change during the life of this guidebook.

For information about all bus and train services in Surrey contact the Surrey Traveline, Passenger Transport Group, Environment, Surrey County Council, County Hall, Kingston upon Thames, Surrey KT1 2DY, telephone (01737) 223000.

Kent County Council publishes an annual Public Transport Map and Guide which contains comprehensive bus and rail route maps and lists of bus services and operators. Public transport information can be obtained from Highways and Transportation Department, Kent County Council, Springfield, Maidstone, Kent ME14 2LQ, telephone (0345) 696996.

For details of train services please telephone either (0345) 484950 or London (0171) 928 5100.

You are advised to check details of your journey before travelling, particularly on Sundays.

Useful addresses and telephone numbers

If you have any comments or suggestions about this or any other recreation route in Surrey please contact the Rights of Way Group, Environment, Surrey County Council, County Hall, Kingston upon Thames KT1 2DY. In Kent please contact the Access and Recreation Officer, Planning Department, Kent County Council, Springfield, Maidstone, Kent ME14 2LX, telephone Maidstone (01622) 696168.

The route should not be obstructed in any way but if it is in Surrey please contact the above address, telephone (0181) 419331.

Path at Shipbourne

The Way at Boughton Monchelsea

In Kent please contact the Public Rights of way Manager, Highways & Transportation Department, Kent County Council, Springfield, Maidstone, Kent ME14 2LQ, telephone Maidstone (01622) 696740.

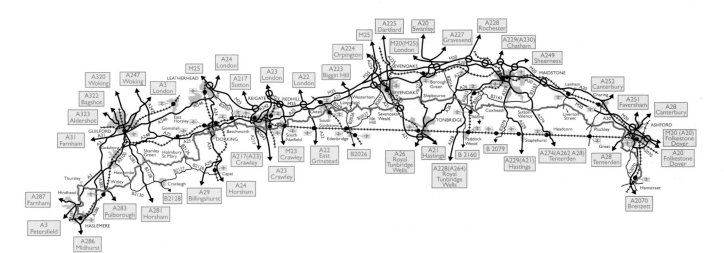

Track at Boughton Malherbe

South East England Tourist Board,
The Old Brew House, Warwick Park, Royal Tunbridge Wells, Kent TN2 5TU,
telephone (01892) 540766.

Guildford:
Tourist Information Centre, 14 Tunsgate, Guildford, Surrey GU1 3QT,
telephone (01483) 44433.

Sevenoaks:
Tourist Information Centre, Buckhurst Lane, Sevenoaks, Kent TN13 1LQ,
telephone (01732) 450305.

Maidstone:
Tourist Information Centre, The Gatehouse, The Old Palace Gardens, Mill Street, Maidstone, Kent ME16 6YE,
telephone (01622) 673581.

Ashford:
Tourist Information Centre, 18 The Churchyard, Ashford, Kent TN23 1QG,
telephone (01233) 629165.

Walkers' organisations
Ramblers' Association,
1/5 Wandsworth Road, London SW8 2XX,
telephone (0171) 339 8500.

Surrey Area Secretary:
Mr G Butler, 109 Selsdon Park Road, South Croydon, Surrey CR2 8JJ.

Kent Area Secretary:
Mr Peter Skipp, 81 New Street Hill, Bromley, Kent BR1 5BA.

Long Distance Walkers' Association Secretary:
Mr Les Maple, 21 Upcroft, Windsor, Berkshire SL4 3NH,
telephone (01753) 866685.

Surrey Area Secretary:
Mr B Haigh, Cherry Tree House, 17 Lower Edgeborough, Guildford, Surrey GU1 2DX,
telephone (01483) 303020.

Kent Area Secretary:
Mr D Sheldrake, 26 Highview, Vigo Village, Meopham, Gravesend, Kent DA13 0RR,
telephone (01732) 823643.

Conservation bodies
Surrey Wildlife Trust,
School Lane, Pirbright, Woking, Surrey GU24 0JN,
telephone (01483) 488055.

Kent Wildlife Trust,
Tyland Barn, Sandling, Maidstone, Kent ME14 3BD,
telephone (01622) 753017.

Countryside Commission,
South East Regional Office,
4th Floor, 71 Kingsway,
London WC2B 6ST,
telephone (0171) 831 3510.

Miscellaneous

Ordnance Survey,
Romsey Road, Maybush,
Southampton,
Hampshire SO9 4DH,
telephone (01703) 792000.

Weathercall
(up-to-date weather forecast)
Surrey and Kent area
(0891) 772 272

P & R Publicity Ltd
(Achievement badges for
most long distance paths)
Queensway, Stem Lane
Industrial Estate, New Milton,
Hampshire BH25 5NN.

Accommodation

There is an abundance of bed
and breakfast establishments
along the Greensand Way (look
for the bed symbol on the route
maps). It is advisable to book
accommodation in advance,
especially in the summer.

Information about
accommodation along the

Cricket at Little Chart Forstal

Greensand Way can be obtained
from the following organisations:

Surrey Tourism,
Leisure and Tourism Unit,
Surrey County Council,
County Hall, Kingston upon
Thames, Surrey KT1 2DT,
telephone (0181) 541 9928.

Kent Tourism,
Economic Development
Department, Kent County
Council, Springfield,
Maidstone, Kent ME14 2LL,
telephone (01622) 696165.

**Mole Valley District
Council,** Pippbrook, Dorking,
Surrey RH4 1SJ,
telephone (01306) 885001.

**South East England Tourist
Board and Guildford,
Sevenoaks, Maidstone and
Ashford Tourist Information
Centres** (listed elsewhere).

Ramblers' Association
The Ramblers' Association (also
listed) publishes the Ramblers'
Year Book and Accommodation
Guide, which is available from
local bookshops.

Youth Hostels
There are three youth hostels on,
or close to, the Greensand Way

Youth Hostels Association,
Trevelyan House,
8 St Stephen's Hill, St Albans,
Hertfordshire AL1 2DY,
telephone (01727) 845047.

Hindhead:
Youth Hostel, Devil's Punch
Bowl, off Portsmouth Road,
Thursley, Surrey GU8 6NS,
telephone (01428) 604285.

Holmbury St Mary:
Youth Hostel, Radnor Lane,
Holmbury St Mary, Dorking,
Surrey RH5 6NW,
telephone (01306) 730777.

Tanners Hatch (2½ miles):
Tanners Hatch, Polesden Lacey,
Dorking, Surrey RH5 6BE,
telephone (01372) 452528.

You may join the Youth Hostels
Association on arrival at the
hostel, but prior booking is
advisable.

Chapter One

THE VILLAGES OF THE GREENSAND RIDGE

Haslemere ~ Gatestreet Farm (Grafham)

The south-west corner of Surrey seemed for a long time a remote and distant region. Londoners who lived only 35 miles away knew little about it. Communications were poor and the roads, until they were turnpiked in the 18th century, were frequently impassable.

When Samuel Pepys travelled from Guildford to Petersfield in 1668 he engaged a guide. William Cobbett travelling on his 'Rural Rides' in the early 19th century brought back accounts of a countryside which was often bleak and lonely.

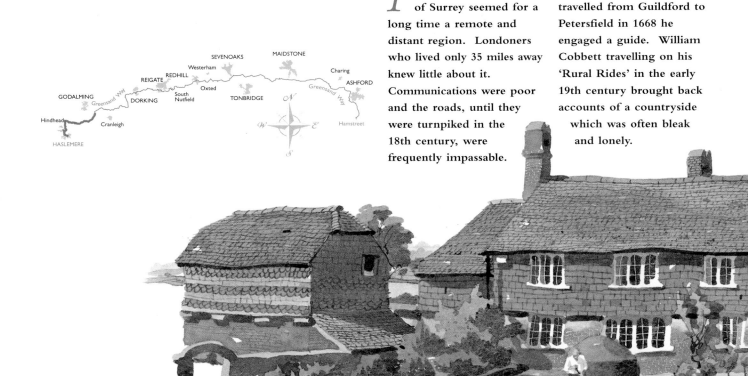

The villages through which the Greensand Way leads you were largely self-contained communities centred on their manors and above all their parish. The chief roads ran from north to south as they radiated from London. Often even the more frequented routes were narrow, sunk deeply in fissures created by weaker lines in the Hythe Beds, while roads linking the villages were few and far between. In addition to farming, most communities developed their own industries as the land allowed; iron and glass in the south-western corner, clothmaking around Witley. Today you can often see reminders in the local place names such as Glasshouse Wood and Kiln Copse below Hambledon. Life was often hard and many people were forced to leave their homes, especially in the mid-19th century.

Ironically this was the time when middle class attitudes changed as intellectual society discovered this countryside and to praise the healthy climate and the open spaces. The coming of the railway in the mid-19th century brought incomers in greater numbers. Numerous houses were built, many to a high specification, and the names of architects such as Norman Shaw, Voysey and Sir Edwin Lutyens occur frequently.

St. Peter's Church, Hambledon

Haslemere

Haslemere grew up as a small market town. In the middle ages it thrived on the local glass-making industry based at Chiddingfold as well as sheep farming on the hills. Ironworks, nearby at Imbhams, provided another living, making guns and shot for His Majesty's stores in the early 17th century. The town was also well-placed to make use of the nearby outcrops of Atherfield clay and both brickworks and pottery works existed. For an introduction to the region it is worth visiting the Haslemere Educational Museum founded in 1888 by Sir Jonathan Hutchinson, a distinguished surgeon at the London Hospital and a resident of the area. The museum includes displays of local natural history and of the local Wealden iron and glass industries.

The 17th and 18th centuries saw some expansion. You will find attractive timbered and tile-hung buildings from this period. The Town Hall, once with arcades at ground level, and the Town House, home for a while of the mountaineer Sir Edward Whymper, are just two. The George Inn was established by 1747. The 19th century saw greater expansion when the railway came in 1859. Later that century Haslemere became a centre for the Arts and Crafts movement.

St Bartholomew's Church is one of many you will find on the Greensand Way where Victorian architects restored and re-ordered churches which had stood for centuries. While the tower survives from the 13th century, this church was largely rebuilt, by J W Penfold, in 1870. A stained glass window in the north aisle by Edward Burne Jones sums up the style of the period. In memory of Alfred, Lord Tennyson who lived at Aldworth near the top of Blackdown, one mile to the south east, it depicts Sir Galahad, from the Arthurian poems the poet wrote there.

As you walk away from the church and the 18th-century buildings around it, you begin to see the architectural develop-ment which started in late Victorian times. One important house is Ballindune, in Weydown Lane, built by E J May in 1905. As you walk on the southern part of Hindhead Common you see others on the far slopes to the east of the Hindhead Road. Here Voysey built one of his finest, New Place, in 1895.

Hindhead Common

Hindhead grew up in the 1880s when John Tyndall, Professor of Engineering, came to live nearby, in search of the fresh air and peace. His home stands on the edge of the Common, the nearby Tyndalls Wood and Tyndalls estate recalling his name. At the time only the inn, The Royal Huts, and a few houses stood along the Portsmouth road. Soon many more houses joined them, built following designs by Norman Shaw. Others away from the main road include houses designed by Lutyens. Conan Doyle came to live here, as did George Bernard Shaw. Of their houses, one is now a preparatory school, the other an hotel.

When the financier Sir Whitaker Wright, owner of much of the common land nearby, was charged with fraud and committed suicide in 1905, developers were keen to rush in and houses might have sprung up over the entire area. Fortunately Hindhead Common, Gibbet Hill and the Devil's Punch Bowl, once the wastes of the manor of Thursley, were among the first tracts of

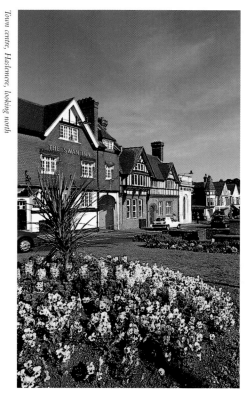

Town centre, Haslemere, looking north

open space bought by the National Trust. Led by Sir Robert Hunter, a founder member of the National Trust and a resident at Haslemere, the public subscribed and so saved the land from development.

Hindhead had for long been the haunt of highwaymen and robbers. The name of Gibbet Hill recalls the death by hanging of three men who in 1786 first befriended an unknown sailor at the Red Lion Public House in Thursley, then murdered him for his purse on their way past the Devil's Punch Bowl. The Celtic Cross, in Cornish granite, was erected in memory of the sailor in 1851.

With such a reputation it is hardly surprising that William Cobbet called the place 'the most villainous spot God ever made'. Today it is hard to believe that description as you stand by the cross and survey the Surrey hills, the scarp face of the Greensand ridge, the Hythe Beds of the Lower Greensand, dropping down into the Weald below. From west to east you see the slopes below Hambledon and the steep slopes of Burgate Hangar; then the trees of the Hurtwood, the high points of Hascombe Hill, Pitch Hill and Leith Hill. To the south you can see the South Downs.

Celtic Cross on Gibbet Hill, Hindhead Common

Above the Devil's Punch Bowl, Hindhead Common

The walk now takes you north, down the route of the old Portsmouth Road, once one of the busiest in England, especially to the north where traffic flowed constantly between Witley and the ironworks at Thursley. The road was turnpiked and improved in the 18th century. The new road was built lower down the hillside in 1826.

Devil's Punch Bowl

The Devil's Punch Bowl may derive its name from the mists which swirl in the low-lying parts, then rise in waves, giving the impression of a punch bowl overflowing with liquid. According to legend the devil hurled a clod of earth at Thor, the god of thunder, who lived

at Thursley, causing a huge hole to appear in the hillside. In reality, the hollow was formed as water emerged from fissures along the spring line where the Hythe Beds rest on the Atherfield clay, its action scouring the slopes. You can see the shale and mudstone deposits of the Atherfield clay in Highcomb Bottom.

The area was cultivated from at least Saxon times. On the far slopes lies Highcomb Copse, where low banks suggest old field boundaries. Remains of charcoal hearths and saw pits have also been found. There are also the more recent foundations of old cottages, once owned by the 'Broom Squires' who made their living selling besoms made from furze.

The heathland supports many plants. Here you will find not only the common heather or ling, but also bell heather and cross-leaved heath. Over the entire Common more than 60 species of birds have been identified. You may even hear the Dartford warbler on the heathland or the wood warbler or redstart in the woodland. On the far slopes you see areas of ancient woodland where trees have been established for at least 400 years. Their high canopy of oak and beech provide an important habitat for wildlife. More common, however, are the areas of secondary woodland where you will see birch, Scots pine, rowan, whitebeam and oak. In places are stands of sweet chestnut coppice. Today, the land is actively managed by the National Trust to conserve the landscape and maintain the habitat. As you walk further down the slope you pass farmhouses which have stood, some since the 16th century, their original timber frames extended and conserved.

Unlike the Hindhead area, Thursley appealed to William Cobbett who described the peaty soil as 'some of the very best barley land in the kingdom'. In the 17th century, using iron from Witley Park and from the Weald, that peat provided fuel for a small iron works at Horsebane Hammer, furnace and forge, (1⅛ mile) north-east of Thursley church. Today the Common is conserved as an important National Nature Reserve.

Thor's Clearing

Thursley, Thunor 'd Leah', may once have been the clearing sacred to Thor. A church has stood since Saxon times on the site where you now find the Church of St Michael and All Angels. Thursley was not in Domesday Book and the church may have been a chapel of ease to Witley. As well as Saxon windows in their original timber frames you will find a Saxon font made from a piece of Bargate Stone, 15th-century stained glass from Germany and a piscina broken, possibly when Roundheads occupied the region in the Civil War of 1642-48. In the churchyard you will find the stone erected in memory of the sailor murdered on Gibbet Hill. Eight fine chest tombs recall more residents of the 18th century, more prosperous in their day than the sailor but less well remembered. When you leave the churchyard it is worth turning left to walk up The Street to see one of the finest collections of domestic buildings in Surrey, including Lutyen's own house at the top.

The parish of Witley

From Thursley the Greensand Way now leads you towards Witley, the other main village in medieval times, for which St Michael's Church served at first as a chapel of ease. At the height of the iron industry it produced enough iron for two forges. The lakes may have been landscaped to infill sites where the ore was excavated.

William Cobbett had visited Witley Park when it was still known as Lea Park and House.

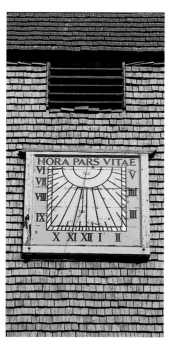

St Michael's and All Saint's Church, Thursley, and clock on shingled tower of church

Step Cottage, Witley

Sir Whitaker Wright, the London financier, renamed it and had it rebuilt in 1890. No expense was spared. The walls, considered at the time 'the finest in England' and which run for six miles round the estate cost £37,000. Wright also spent £840,000 on the mansion and £500,000 on the landscaping. Witley House was built in neo-Tudor style by H.Paxton Watson. Lutyens also worked on it for a while

Brook, another hamlet, like Bowlhead Green, is now considered a part of Witley. The Dog and Pheasant, 500 yards to the south on the A286, was once a Wealden hall house, its fireplace in the centre of the hall. A road had run from early times along the line of the A286 and the turnpike opened over Wormley Hill in 1762. It was a favourite route for carriers bringing fish up from the south coast, especially from Shoreham, for the London markets.

Witley village, three miles to the north-east, on the A283, is well worth a visit. An important parish in medieval times, it exercised considerable influence over the region. It was for several centuries a centre for the wool and textile industry in the South East. The village contains a number of attractive houses, some dating

King Edward's School, Wormley

from the 16th century. Step Cottage is one of the best, with half-timbering and hung tiles. The Church of All Saints is one of only a few in Surrey which contain Saxon stone work. You can also see some superb frescoes from the 12th century on the south wall. The White Hart was built in the 16th century on the site of an old hunting lodge

Nostalgia

The advent of coal in the north of England brought an end to the iron industry in the south, and the conversion of the mills to cloth-working. Witley's industry was well in decline when the small hamlet at Sandhills became a centre for intellectuals in the late 19th century. J C Hart built Pinewood, the first house, there. Among others lived the artist Helen Allingham whose paintings of cottages here and elsewhere, in bright clear light helped to preserve a sentimental view of an already vanishing country life style. George Eliot lived nearby at The Heights outside Witley. At that time the area was still heavily wooded and must have had an air of great seclusion.

Wormley, one mile south of Witley, first grew up around the railway, which cut through the thick woodland. Opened on 24 January 1859, it was known as Witley for Chiddingfold until 1947. The village grew further from 1867, when King Edward's School was founded, for '240 destitute children of both sexes.'

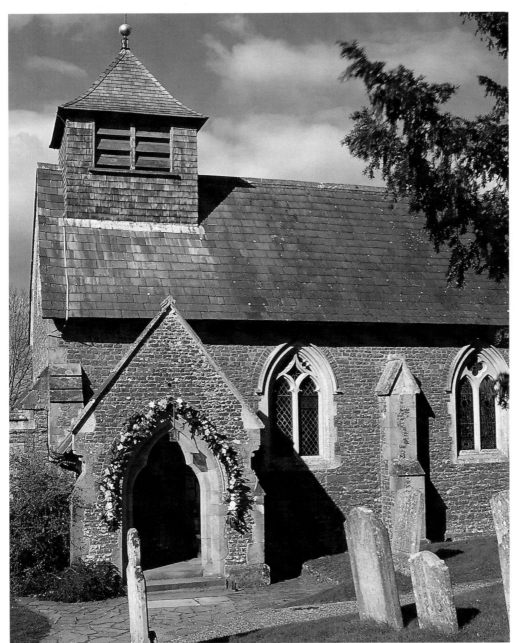

Porch and tower at St Peter's Church, Hambledon

As you climb up to Hambledon Common there are several reminders that the idyll seen by the intellectuals of Sandhills had not always applied to everyone. The building which still bears the name of the Royal Oceanographic Institute served as the Union Workhouse, built in 1786. It was later to become the 'Hambledon Homes'. Hambledon Common itself provided a refuge for men, women and children on their journey north from Petworth on the Chartist marches of 1838.

Around Hambledon are reminders of past industry, as the name of fields and copses make clear. Glasshouse and Kiln occur frequently to the south and Blunden's Wood contains the site of an important medieval glass works. Within the village stands Oakhurst Cottage. This houses the Gertrude Jekyll collection of West Surrey ´Bygones'. An important collection, it gives some idea of the style of life lived before the turn of the century. Gertrude Jekyll, the gardener and collaborator in design with Lutyens, studied the people of west Surrey at the turn of the century, observing the details of their lifestyle, their houses, furniture and implements and wrote her account in 'Old West Surrey'. In so doing she was able to preserve some of the reality, as opposed to the picturesque scenes portrayed by artists such as Helen Allingham and Miles Burkett Foster.

Rosebay willow herb

Today Hambledon is a conservation area. Many of its buildings are half-timbered or have hung tiles. The area around St Peter's Church is particularly attractive, with tile-hung Court Farm and granary nearby, as is Malthouse Lane, where you find Malthouse Farmhouse and Malthouse Cottage, both built in the 17th century. A noticeable feature here is the galleting in the walls, where chips of ironstone found in layers of the Sandgate Beds are placed in the mortar. Various stories appear to explain this practice. According to legend the chips keep the devil

away. In reality they help to stabilise the roughly hewn Bargate stone. Incidentally they also prevent the birds pecking at the mortar. Lutyens drew on much he saw here for his own work, recreating the old features in his designs as in his most notable house of all, Tigbourne Court, near Witley. This is built in Bargate stone with galleting as here.

Before this, the Celts...

In the first century Iron Age Celts chose the spur above the village of Hascombe to establish a hill fort, one in a line of several along the top of the scarp face. Overlooking the Weald it offered them good defence in case of attack, while enabling them to pursue their search for iron ore. The valley was settled from Saxon times but the village of Hascombe remained isolated well into the last century. The road through it boasted a milestone and a toll-house but was still one that William Cobbett considered

impassable. The White Horse Inn has stood beside the road since the 17th century. In the latter part of the 19th century the village began to attract people who sought the calm of Surrey and later Lutyens was to build a number of villas on the slopes.

The Greensand Way takes you past The White Horse and along Church Lane, where you will see the Church of St Peter, rebuilt by Henry Woodyer in 1864. Replacing a much older church which had a wooden tower, as was traditional in the

county, this is generally considered to be one of the finest Victorian reconstructions in Surrey. The redesigned chancel roof represents an upturned fishing boat. A stained glass window depicting the patron saint continues the fishing theme. The village pond has served as both fish pond and millpond in its time. Shown as marshy land on maps at the turn of the century, it is now fully restored.

The White Horse inn sign and lane, Hascombe

Leith Hill Tower, the highest point in south-east England

Chapter Two

LAND FOR THE PEOPLE

Gatestreet Farm (Grafham) ~ Deepdene (Dorking)

The Way now takes you through Bramley Parish, through woodland past Selhurst Common and over the old estate of Wintershall to Shamley Green. From there you make your way to Winterfold Heath and climb a series of hills which dominate the scarp. Reynards Hill, Pitch Hill, Holmbury Hill and Leith Hill all give breathtaking views over the Weald. On the clearest days there is even the occasional glimpse of the English Channel. In between Holmbury Hill and Leith Hill lies the village of Holmbury St Mary, formed as a parish centre in the 19th century when two small hamlets were united by the building of St Mary's Church. A steady walk down the dip slope takes you along Broadmoor Bottom, through more woodland and alongside the River Tillingbourne first near Broadmoor, then through old parkland to the Pipp Brook. From then the Way leads you on the slopes above the Gault clay valley along the Upper Greensand. The North Downs rise nearby as you walk through Westcott and towards Dorking.

Woodland restored

In a county already renowned for its cover of trees the slopes above Hascombe are especially well-wooded. More often than not this is the result of a return to woodland, rather than an unbroken sequence of natural growth and regeneration. Old manors often ran southwards, narrow and wedge-shaped, from the fertile clay valley to the north. The southern, upper slopes of the Hythe Beds, above the scarp, were far less fertile. From medieval times they had formed part of the manorial wastes where commoners could gather timber for building their houses, for firewood and bracken for their bedding. They could also graze their sheep or pigs. Grazed over centuries, any natural goodness in the soil was leached out and a new heathland ground cover emerged.

Hindhead Common is one such as this. Now the Greensand Way takes you over many more stretches that once were common land. They are not always recognisable as such. In some places secondary woodland has grown up, in others plantations of pine and softwood appear, some of them centuries old. In other places modern conservation techniques are restoring the heathland environment.

Countryside for all

Valuable too are the stretches given at the turn of the century so that the public could enjoy the land. This was part of a general trend which had begun in the 1870s when people became aware of the value of the remaining 'wastes'. All through the 19th century various Enclosure Acts had allowed landowners to appropriate the common land for their own use, whether it was for cultivation or for building development. As well as intellectuals settling in these further parts of Surrey, ordinary working people of all classes came here to walk and later to cycle. The spaces took on a new value, this time for recreation.

The response was strong. Not only did large bodies such as the National Trust help to preserve the open spaces for the people. Individuals too gave land. Leith Hill, as well as The Nower and the Glory Wood on either side of Dorking, are prime examples of land once in private ownership that all can now enjoy.

From the village of Hascombe the Greensand Way takes you across land which for several centuries in late medieval times was the home of the Wintershull family. It is an example of the way estates were gradually divided up into smaller parcels of land. The manor of Wintershull separated from Bramley in early 13th century and the same family

held it until the beginning of the 17th century. Selhurst Common, once part of that land, is now covered with secondary woodland. There are peaty areas in the hollow. A flush of bluebells covers the slopes in the spring.

Canals and railways

The broad valley where today the A281 runs used to see oak carted north from the area round Cranleigh in vast quantities. As on most roads in Surrey the going was often difficult for, in general, the small towns and villages suffered from poor communications. The rough condition of roads hampered transport of commodities and so hindered development. A canal had first been built on the River Wey in the 17th century, running from the confluence of the Thames and the Wey as far as Guildford. This was extended to Godalming in 1763. In the early 19th century the Earl of Egremont, who lived at Petworth, poured much of his fortune into improving agriculture. With his backing a canal was built to link the Wey Navigation with that of the Arun. The Wey and Arun

Canal rose by seven locks to Cranleigh, then descended by 16 locks to Loxwood and Newbridge. The canal was not a commercial success and closed down in 1871. Today the old locks may be identified by just a few portions of old timbers.

The old railway, opened in 1865 and closed exactly 100 years later under the Beeching axe, has a more useful fate, serving as the line of the Downs Link long-distance bridleway.

At Shamley Green, attractively set around a large Green, houses dating from at least the 17th century are reminders of a once self-sufficient community. The house names, such as Barn Cottage, The Old Forge, and, on the slopes above, Tanyard Farm, give clear indication of their working past. Plonks Farm may possibly have been built from planks of wood, rather than heavy timbers, while Shamley Green itself, once Shamble Lane, may go back even further, recalling a Saxon word for the shelf of land on which the village lies.

Hurtwood escarpment after the 1987 storm

Towards the Hurtwood

You now pass a number of outlying farms such as Stroud Farm, Franklin's and 18th-century Willinghurst, then climb steadily uphill to Winterfold Heath and Winterfold Hill. This was once common land, which once provided reasonable protection for winter grazing. Today it is part of the Hurtwood, a large area which takes its name from the hurts, bilberries or whortleberries which grow on the sandy hills crossed by the walk. The largest part of the Hurtwood lies in the manor of Shere cum Vachery, which has been held by the Bray family since Tudor times. In 1926 Sir Reginald Bray granted this land to the public to give people 'the right to air and exercise'. Including land from several parishes, the Bray estate is the largest area of privately owned common land in Surrey. It is now managed by the Hurtwood Control Committee to achieve a balance between good forestry, conservation and recreation.

It is probable that at the time of Domesday Book the woods on Pitch Hill were mixed oak woods, whose acorns supported

Toposcope & Memorial, Pitch Hill

many pigs. The first Scots pines were planted by William Bray in 1770. The open land was heathland with a mixture of grass, heather and bilberries. Today an attractive feature is the spread of the Amelanchier lamarckii, or juneberry, imported from America, which has naturalised on the slopes.

Leith Hill

Leith Hill is the highest point along the Greensand ridge. At 967 feet it is the highest point in south-east England. In the mid-18th century Royal Engineers surveying the country claimed to see 41 London churches. Many of those have now gone but the panorama is still extensive. In the 17th century Richard Hull, esquire, of Leith Hill Place gained permission from the Evelyn family of Wotton who owned the land to build a prospect tower based on the design of an early 14th-century Wealden

tower and bring the elevation to something over 1,000 feet. From the top Richard Hull and his friends viewed the countryside, with telescopes to enhance the view, seated on chairs he had brought up for their comfort. Hull was buried, at his own request, beneath the tower. In 1863 the Evelyn family resumed possession of the tower and added the octagonal turret, the spiral staircase and the parapet, bringing the total elevation to 1,029 feet.

Today the tower and the Leith Hill estate covering 860 acres are owned and managed by the National Trust, an accumulation of land and property as gifts over the last 70 years by previous owners.

The tower and five acres of land came to them in 1923 from W J MacAndrew. Ralph Vaughan Williams, the composer, gave Leith Hill Place and 400 acres of land in 1945. The rhododendrons in his old gardens are still a blaze of colour in spring. Public subscription enabled the Trust to purchase nearby Duke's Warren and Severell's Copse in 1931. Other individuals gave more land while the Trust purchased Coldharbour Common to the east in 1986.

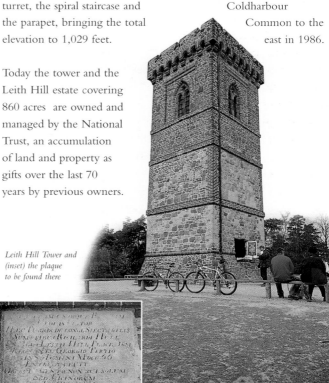

Leith Hill Tower and (inset) the plaque to be found there

Much of Leith Hill is an SSSI, protecting several important wildlife habitats. On the slopes below the tower lies Leith Hill Place Woods, one of the few areas where ancient semi-natural woodland has survived, and now a home for breeding woodpeckers, warblers and redstarts as well as for several rare moths. Tits, goldcrests and finches also frequent the area.

Slopes restored

Most of the plateau and the northern slopes have been stripped of their original timber. Constant grazing and foraging by the commoners had combined with the enormous demand for fuel made by the iron industry and, later, gunpowder manufacture. On the plateau itself, to the north, you will find areas of secondary woodland which have grown up in the last 100 years, since grazing began to decline. Here you will find Scots pine, holly and rowan as well as oak and birch. In early summer the whitebeam are especially attractive with their downy leaves upturned. Some patches of the heathland still remain with ling, bell heather and bilberry (known locally as hurts)

The Cascade (Tillingbourne Falls) near Broadmoor.

among the heather, and today the National Trust is working to conserve this where possible, balancing the needs of wildlife throughout the estate.

From Leith Hill you turn northwards and walk down the slopes of the Duke's Warren and

along Broadmoor Bottom near the Tilling Springs, where one branch of the River Tillingbourne starts its journey towards the River Wey. The Duke's Warren, once used for hunting, was planted between 1870 and 1880 with spruce firs for commercial growth. When

the timber came to maturity and was felled during the First World War a railway track ran the length of Broadmoor valley to transport the logs.

The re-growth of trees on the slopes today would have delighted John Evelyn, diarist, founder member of the Royal Society and writer on the landscape. He grew up in the 17th century on the Wotton estate to the north. This had been owned by members of the Evelyn family from the late 16th century. Much of the family's fortune had been made through their iron mill at Abinger, the most northerly forge in Surrey. Timber and water were available here and transport of the finished product to London was easier. The pig iron used was brought here from further south. Later the Evelyn family established gunpowder, brass and iron mills.

Conservation in the 17th century

As everywhere else throughout the South East, the iron industry flourished at the expense of the old woodland. Gradually people became aware of the devastation caused by the consumption of timber. In 1560, before the Evelyns came, this was already a protected area and loud complaints were raised against an earlier iron worker who claimed he had a licence and felled 1200 beech and oak in one year. By the 17th century there were many more complaints.

John Evelyn grew up with a deep affection for the countryside around him which he retained during extensive travels elsewhere in England, and in Europe. Evelyn described the slopes above the Tillingbourne with affection:

'It was sweetly environ'd with those delicious and venerable woods, as in the judgment of strangers as of Englishmen, it may be compared to one of the most tempting and pleasant seates in the Nation.'

Evelyn took a great interest in the landscape and was one of the first to write about the planting of trees. His 'Sylva', a 'Discourse of Forest-trees, and the Propagation of Timber', was a description of the various kinds of trees, their cultivation, and uses. It undoubtedly influenced the 18th-century trend to re-

establish woodland, especially the Scots pine you see on the slopes of the Greensand ridge.

Westcott

The village of Westcott, next to the A25, has always stood beside a busy route. Fortunately it survived a plan of the 1940s to expand it to a small town and today is part of a conservation area. Some houses survive from the 17th century but most were built in the Surrey vernacular style of the late 19th century and early 20th century. Holy Trinity Church on the slopes above the main road was designed by Sir George Gilbert Scott, one of the most prolific architects of Victorian times whose numerous designs in the Gothic Revival style include the Albert Memorial and the Midland, later St Pancras', Hotel. Holy Trinity Church fits perfectly into the setting, with shingled spire and ragstone walls.

Holy Trinity Church, Westcott

The Temple on The Nower

The Nower and the Glory Wood

The Nower forms part of a stretch of sandy heathland and woodland which was given to Dorking by Lt Col R W Barclay in 1931. Today it is conserved both for its landscape value and ecological value and as an amenity. First mentioned in 1247 as the land of Osbert del Ore, it was enclosed before 1870 by Edward Walter who built the Bury Hill Estate. As common land it had been well grazed and the woodland has grown up in the last 100 years. The trees are dense, their species varied, at many different stages of growth. You will find, beneath the dense canopy, younger and smaller trees such as elder, hazel and holly while

in the undergrowth speedwell and stitchwort can be found as well as a host of bluebells in season. The dead wood encourages insects and, as a result, many birds nest here. You may hear green, greater spotted and lesser spotted woodpeckers, owls and nuthatches, among others birds.

On the far side of Dorking the Glory Wood, too, has grown up within the last 100 years. A favourite resort of Dorking people in the late 19th century, it was presented to the people of Dorking in 1928 by the Duke of Newcastle. Beech now dominates the woods but there are some fine glimpses of the North Downs which continue to be a strong feature along the Way.

Windmill on Reigate Heath

Chapter Three

INDUSTRY PAST AND PRESENT

Deepdene (Dorking) ~ Oxted Place

The Way now leaves the heathland and the woods of the Hythe Beds and through the Lower Greensand and takes you from Deepdene on the outskirts of Dorking, though Betchworth Park to the village of Brockham, and alongside the River Mole to Betchworth. From there you walk to Reigate Park and Reigate Hill, and on to Earlswood Common. Today this is a pleasant open space, but once was marked with kilns and clay pits, for long a scene of brick-making. Next you move on to South Nutfield, where old workings now provide a home for wildlife, then make your way up to Castle Hill below Bletchingley, where a thriving medieval market town is now an attractive village. You continue below Tilburstow Hill, past Godstone and so move on to Tandridge where the last of the fullers earth remains below the ground.

Deepdene

At first through Deepdene and Betchworth Park you walk across land that was once garden or landscaped park. The area of Deepdene, to the south-east of Dorking, takes its name from one of the country's most outstanding houses and gardens. In 1655 John Evelyn visited and described the earlier house, built in 1652 by Charles Howard. He was impressed by its gardens '...a solitary recess being 15 acres, environed by a hill.' The garden contained rare plants, with cherries, myrtles, orange trees. In the next century, the Duke of Norfolk, a descendent of the first owner, built a new house in Palladian style.

This was replaced from 1807 by Thomas Hope, a prolific writer on art and architecture, from 1807 and an avid collector of paintings. Hope combined nature and romanticism with the formal style, and built a semi-circular porch, battlements and a tower. It was this third version of the house, set in magnificent gardens which brought particular delight. The many visitors whom Thomas Hope and his son Henry attracted included Benjamin Disraeli who wrote his novel 'Coningby' here. In the 20th century Deepdene fell into disrepair and was demolished in 1969.

As you walk up the slope to the east of the A24 which now bisects the estate you see the old rhododendron terraces.

These are now being conserved and restored by Mole Valley District Council as part of the work to clear and replant the area after the 1987 storm. Park Farmhouse on the edge of Betchworth Park, once known as Home Farmhouse, was first built in the 1550s, and became the home farm for Deepdene. Red brick and tiles cover the original timber framing.

The River Mole, near Brockham

Brockham

At Brockham you leave open, agricultural land and come to a village, set around the village green. Until the A25 was built in 1927 Brockham was one of a line of coaching stations on the old Reigate road which passed through the village but now it is a peaceful place. First you pass the village pump, a listed building, This stands over a disused spring as a memorial to Henry Hope who gave the land on which the church was built.

Before Christ Church was built, on the far side of the green, villagers had to walk to church in Betchworth one mile away. In the mid-19th century Henry Goulburn MP who owned the manor, provided money for a church in memory of his son. Benjamin Ferrey was the architect, a pupil of the architect Pugin and designer of many other churches in Surrey. A local landowner, Sir Benjamin Brodie gave carefully selected stone from quarries on his land at Betchworth and the building was completed in 1846. Successive vicars waged war with cattle from the Green which constantly strayed into the church until a committee took charge in 1868.

The River Mole, which rises north Sussex near Rusper, flows, with many tributaries, 50 miles to the Thames at Molesey. Like the Tillingbourne and the Pipp Brook which flow into it, it once powered numerous mills

One small watermill appears on a 1634 map of the Brockham manor while at Betchworth a mill may have been used for fulling as early as 1299.

Betchworth

A church has stood on the site of St Michael's, Betchworth, since Domesday times, while an inn is said to have stood as long as the church itself. The present inn, The Dolphin, built in the 18th century, may take its name from the French Dauphin, later Louis IX, who came to support King John in his wars against the Barons. As you leave the churchyard you find an attractive collection of old buildings, the gateway to the churchyard, the Old Mill Cottage and The Old Forge.

The church contains several interesting memorials, two to Royal surgeons. One was Thomas Morsted, doctor to Henry IV, Henry V and Henry VI. He travelled with the English army of Henry V. When he died he left an annuity of 16 pennies for repair of the church. The other, honoured with a bust and a marble plaque in the south nave, was to Sir Benjamin Brodie, who lived at Broome Park. The owner of stone pits, and donor of stone for churches, Sir Benjamin was doctor to William IV and Victoria and enjoyed an international reputation as an orthopaedic surgeon.

Priest's cottage and church gate, Betchworth churchyard

Greensand Way Questionnaire

In order to help us assess the success of the Greensand Way, we would like to hear your views about the route and the guidebook.

Please would you complete the questionnaire below and send it to the Access and Recreation Officer, Planning Department, Kent County Council, Springfield, Maidstone, Kent ME14 2LX. If you have borrowed this book from a library or friend, you may photocopy the questionnaire.

1. Which of these statements best describes you?

I live close to the Greensand Way ☐

I came to this area of Kent specifically to walk the Greensand Way ☐

I did not come to this area of Kent specifically to walk the Greensand Way ☐

2. Name of town/village where you live (include post code):

....

....

3. How did you first become aware of the Greensand Way?

Leaflet (which one) ☐

....

Word-of-mouth ☐

Saw sign or waymark ☐

Advertising (where) ☐

....

Newspaper (which one)

....

Other (write in)

....

4. What influenced you to try the Greensand Way apart from liking walking?

....

....

....

....

....

....

5. Have you, or do you intend to:

Walk all of the route in one go, or over a short period of time (eg. one week) ☐

Walk all of the route, in sections, over a longer period of time ☐

Walk only sections of the route ☐

Unlikely to walk any part of the route ☐

6. Which of the following modes of travel do you use to get to the start of your walk?

Walk ☐

Bus ☐

Cycle ☐

Train ☐

Car ☐

Other (write in) ☐

....

....

7. If you found the walk difficult to follow, what improvements would you like us to make, and where (please use grid references where possible)?

....

....

....

....

....

....

....

....

8. Please indicate the number of people in each category that accompanied you on your walk (including you).

Age	Male	Female
Under 11	☐	☐
11–16	☐	☐
17–25	☐	☐
26–35	☐	☐
36–45	☐	☐
46–55	☐	☐
56–65	☐	☐
Over 65	☐	☐

Haven't done the walk yet ☐

9. Would you recommend the Greensand Way to anyone else?

Yes ☐

No ☐

If you answered "no" please tell us why you say that:

....

....

....

10. Where did you obtain this guidebook from?

Bookshop ☐

Multiple retailer (eg. W H Smith) ☐

Other shop (write in type) ☐

....

Tourist information centre ☐

Library ☐

Mail Order ☐

11. What do you like about the guidebook?

....

....

....

....

....

....

....

....

....

Is there anything you dislike about the guidebook?

....

....

....

....

....

....

....

....

....

12. How useful did you find the detachable route maps?

Easy to read and understand ☐

Satisfactory ☐

Difficult to follow ☐

Don't know ☐

13. Have you walked any section of these other routes?

North Downs Way ☐

Saxon Shore Way ☐

Wealdway ☐

Darent Valley Path ☐

Stour Valley Walk ☐

Elham Valley Way ☐

Medway Valley Walk ☐

Eden Valley Walk ☐

High Weald Walk ☐

Along and Around the Greensand Way

Haslemere - Westerham - Hamstreet

route guide

and footpath maps
including Ordnance Survey maps

ROUTE GUIDE ~ CONTENTS

Cover illustration:
View of Bough Beech Reservoir
from Hanging Bank

ROUTE MAP INFORMATION

The route maps are reproduced from the Ordnance Survey Pathfinder Series enlarged to a scale of 3 ½ inches to 1 mile (5.5 cm to 1 km)

The maps are aligned north/south on each page, and the scale appears on each map spread.

All sections of the walk follow legally defined rights of way unless otherwise indicated on route maps. Before using the route guide, walkers are advised to study the key to the route maps and map symbols.

Route directions

Route directions are given for walking the route in an easterly direction only. The route can be walked in a westerly direction using the route map and waymarking alone.

Because the countryside is constantly changing with buildings and natural features appearing and disappearing, and stiles, gates and field boundaries being removed or new ones erected, the route directions may be affected during the life of the guidebook. If in doubt study the route map and follow the signs and waymarks.

Distances and times

The distance and times for each sub-section of the route are shown on the map spreads.

The distances in this guidebook are given in miles. The exact conversion of miles to kilometres is 1 mile to 1.6093 km. For convenience the approximate conversion is 1 mile to 1.6 km.

Conversion table

1 mile	–	1.6 km
2 miles	–	3.2 km
5 miles	–	8 km
10 miles	–	16.1 km

Waymarking and signing

Waymarking

The Greensand Way waymarks are used to show the line of the route in the countryside. You will see them fixed to waymark posts, or posts of gates or stiles. The walk has been waymarked in such a way that it is possible to walk the route in either direction.

In Surrey the route is waymarked by circular waymark discs with GW in the centre of the directional arrow. These are yellow on black for a public foot-path and blue on white for a public bridleway. The few public byways on route have plain red arrows and brown signs (see below).

In Kent the route is waymarked by circular waymark discs with an oast house in the centre of the directional arrow. These are yellow on white for a public footpath, blue on white for a public bridleway and red on white for a public byway.

See page 18 of the guidebook section for detailed information about the waymarking system.

Changes to the route may occur during the life of this guidebook, in which case look out for the diversion signs and follow the waymarks and signs.

Signing

In Surrey where the Greensand Way crosses or leaves a metalled road there are small brown and white Greensand Way notices attached to wooden public footpath, bridleway or byway signposts indicating that the Greensand Way follows the signed route.

In Kent where the Greensand Way crosses or leaves a metalled road there are metal signs fixed to lamp-posts or other posts. The logo is added to the footpath, bridleway or byway signs or used on its own where the route follows a section of road.

Distance check list

This list will assist you in calculating the distances between places on the Greensand Way when checking your progress along the way.

There are three maps in each section of the route. The mileages are sub-divided accordingly.

Route Maps		Distance from the previous location (miles)	Accumulative distance (miles)
1	Haslemere	15½	15½
2	Gatestreet Farm	17½	33
3	Deepdene	18	51
4	Oxted Place	18	69
5	Shipbourne Common	16	85
6	Sutton Valence	14	99
7	Godinton Park	9	108
	Hamstreet		

KEY TO ROUTE MAPS AND SYMBOLS

Key to Ordnance Survey map symbols

Roads and paths

════════	Motorway
────────	Road
────────	Other road, drive or track

Unfenced roads and tracks are shown by pecked lines

....	Path

Railways

────────	Multiple track
────────	Cutting
────────	Embankment
────────	Tunnel
────────	Road over and under
────────	Level crossing and station

Boundaries

─ · ─ · ─	County
─ ─ ─ ─	District
·············	Civil Parish

Symbols

♦	} Church or Chapel {	with tower
♠		with spire
+		without tower or spire
▦		Glasshouse
Λ		Beacon
△		Triangulation station
○ BP, BS		Boundary post/stone
· T, A, R		Telephone: public, AA, RAC
· MP, MS		Mile post/stone
VILLA		Roman antiquity (AD 43 to AD 420)
Castle		Other antiquities
⊹		Site of antiquity
⚔ 1066		Site of battle (with date)

Gravel pit

Sand pit

Chalk pit, clay pit or quarry

Refuse or slag heap

Sloping wall

pylon   pole   Electricity transmission line

○ W, Spr   Well, spring

Sand, sand & shingle

NT   National Trust

Vegetation

Coniferous trees	
Non-coniferous trees	
Coppice	
Orchard	
Scrub	
Bracken, rough grassland	
Heath	
Reeds	
Marsh	
Saltings	

Heights

50 ·   Surface heights are to the nearest metre above mean sea level.

Contours are not shown

GODALMING   Wonersh
Map 2a
10&11   Map 2b
12&
Greensand Way
Milford   Map 1c
8&9
Hindhead   Map 1b   Cranleigh
6&7
Map 1a   Chiddingfold
4&5
HASLEMERE

Key to route map symbols

———	Greensand Way – signed and waymarked
– – –	Link route (access point) – signed and waymarked
–·– ·	Alternative route – signed and waymarked
–·· – ··	Optional access or detour – not signed or waymarked
·····	Other public rights of way
Ⓒ→	Route direction number
7	Interesting feature
page 10	Route map continuation
AW 168	Right of way number

60	Ordnance Survey grid number
	River
	Sea, pond or lake
15	Miles from Haslemere
⇌	Railway station
🚌	Bus route
P	Car parking
☎	Telephone
i	Tourist information
WC	Toilet
🛏	Accommodation

yha	Youth hostel
	Public house
✕	Pub food
🍴	Café/restaurant
☕	Refreshments
	Picnic site
	Foodstore
↓	View point
⚠	Caution – take care

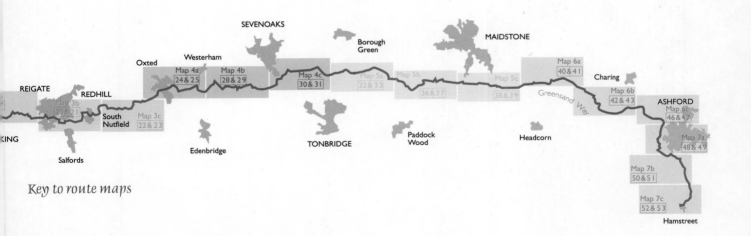

Key to route maps

SEVENOAKS · Westerham · Oxted · Borough Green · MAIDSTONE · Charing · REIGATE · REDHILL · South Nutfield · Salfords · Edenbridge · TONBRIDGE · Paddock Wood · Headcorn · ASHFORD · Hamstreet · KING

Map 3b 20&21 · Map 3c 22&23 · Map 4a 24&25 · Map 4b 28&29 · Map 4c 30&31 · Map 5a 32&33 · Map 5b · Map 5c 38&39 · 36&37 · Map 6a 40&41 · Map 6b 42&43 · Map 6c 46&47 · Map 7a 48&49 · Map 7b 50&51 · Map 7c 52&53

Greensand Way

Haslemere Town Hall

HINDHEAD
all facilities
except ⇌

A3
Guildford
12½ miles

HINDHEAD

HASLEMERE C P

A286 (A3)
Guildford
13½ miles

HASLEMERE
all facilities

0   1 Kilometre   1 Mile

© Crown Copyright. LA076708/97/05

N

Section One

THE VILLAGES OF THE GREENSAND RIDGE

Haslemere ~ Gatestreet Farm (Grafham)

Map 1a

Haslemere (SU 905328) ~ Gibbet Hill (SU 899360)
3¼ miles, allow 1½ hours

Route directions

A From the old Town Hall in Haslemere walk along the left side of the High Street (A286 to Guildford). Twenty five yards past The Georgian Hotel turn left between buildings and follow the footpath to Church Lane.

B Cross the road and turn left over the railway bridge. Bear right at the triangle below St Bartholomew's Church, then continue up High Lane for 250 yards. At Ventnor, cross to the left side of the road, then bear right, up a narrow path, between fences. Cross the road, go over a stile and take the field path downhill.

C Turn left along Bunch Lane for 100 yards, then turn right, up Stoatley Hollow. Bear left beside farm buildings and continue uphill. Bear right, beside Puckfold, onto a rough, semi-metalled track. Turn right at the T-junction, and continue for 380 yards.

D Bear left opposite Little Scotstoun. Follow the path through woodland and over heath, then go steeply downhill for 650 yards ignoring all side tracks. Cross a broad track in the valley bottom. Go ahead uphill. At the top continue ahead, skirting gardens. At a junction of tracks take the central track ahead. Continue almost to the road (A3).

E Turn back through 45 degrees. Follow a broad, sandy track across Hindhead Common for 710 yards. At a seat beneath trees, leave the main track to bear left uphill. Cross an open space where five ways meet. Continue ahead to cross the car park, then walk ahead over Gibbet Hill, leaving the triangulation point and the Celtic Cross to your right.

Interesting features

1 **Haslemere**
The town remained small and isolated until the 19th century. Old maps show clusters of houses only around the High Street and St Bartholomew's Church.

2 **Town Hall**
Originally built in the 17th century, the Town Hall was rebuilt in a similar style in 1814. It used to have arcades, with the ground floor open.

3 **High Street**
In the High Street the Town House, with Doric doorcase, dates from 1725. Sir Edward Whymper, first to climb the Matterhorn, once lived here.

4 **Haslemere Educational Museum**
Sir Jonathan Hutchinson, a distinguished surgeon at the London Hospital, founded this museum in 1888.

5 **Church Hill House**
The walls and gate piers of this 18th-century house are listed monuments as well as the Queen Anne-style house itself. Church Hill Gate was once the stables.

6 **St Bartholomew's Church**
The church tower dates from the 13th century. The rest of the church was rebuilt in the late 19th century. A window by Burne-Jones commemorates the poet Tennyson who lived on Blackdown one mile away.

7 **Hindhead**
The Royal Huts, an old coaching inn, survives from the days when Hindhead was a small staging post on the London to Portsmouth road.

8 **Gibbet Hill**
The Celtic Cross, made of Cornish granite, marks the place where three robbers were hanged on 24 September 1776, for the murder of an unknown sailor on the London to Portsmouth road.

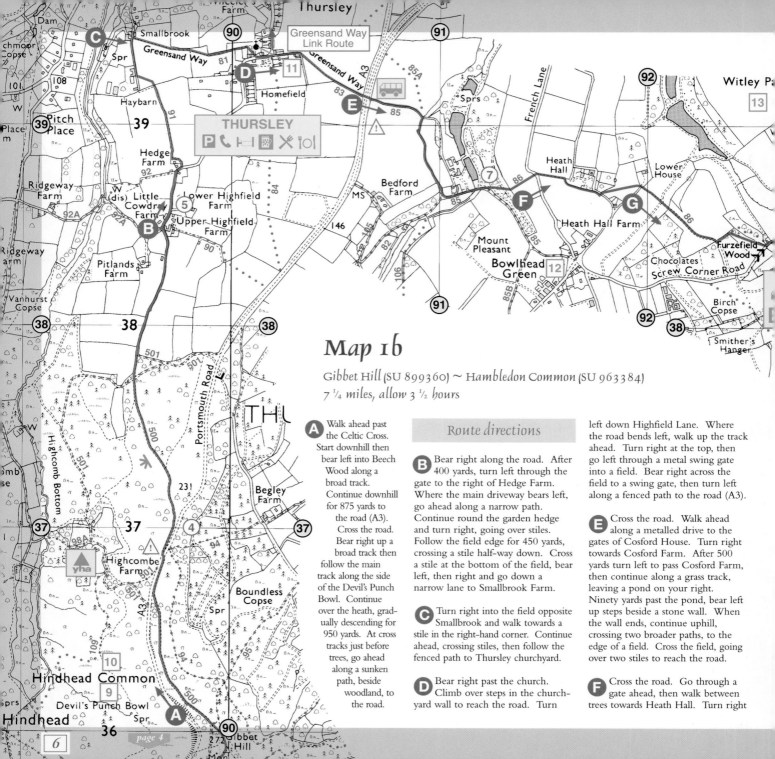

Map 1b

Gibbet Hill (SU 899360) ~ Hambledon Common (SU 963384)
7 ¼ miles, allow 3 ½ hours

Route directions

A Walk ahead past the Celtic Cross. Start downhill then bear left into Beech Wood along a broad track. Continue downhill for 875 yards to the road (A3). Cross the road. Bear right up a broad track then follow the main track along the side of the Devil's Punch Bowl. Continue over the heath, gradually descending for 950 yards. At cross tracks just before trees, go ahead along a sunken path, beside woodland, to the road.

B Bear right along the road. After 400 yards, turn left through the gate to the right of Hedge Farm. Where the main driveway bears left, go ahead along a narrow path. Continue round the garden hedge and turn right, going over stiles. Follow the field edge for 450 yards, crossing a stile half-way down. Cross a stile at the bottom of the field, bear left, then right and go down a narrow lane to Smallbrook Farm.

C Turn right into the field opposite Smallbrook and walk towards a stile in the right-hand corner. Continue ahead, crossing stiles, then follow the fenced path to Thursley churchyard.

D Bear right past the church. Climb over steps in the churchyard wall to reach the road. Turn left down Highfield Lane. Where the road bends left, walk up the track ahead. Turn right at the top, then go left through a metal swing gate into a field. Bear right across the field to a swing gate, then turn left along a fenced path to the road (A3).

E Cross the road. Walk ahead along a metalled drive to the gates of Cosford House. Turn right towards Cosford Farm. After 500 yards turn left to pass Cosford Farm, then continue along a grass track, leaving a pond on your right. Ninety yards past the pond, bear left up steps beside a stone wall. When the wall ends, continue uphill, crossing two broader paths, to the edge of a field. Cross the field, going over two stiles to reach the road.

F Cross the road. Go through a gate ahead, then walk between trees towards Heath Hall. Turn right then follow the field edge for 220 yards. Turn left, down steps, to a lane.

woodland to your right, then bear left into a field and continue for 600 yards along the field edge, again with woodland on your right. Go down steps to the road and continue for 70 yards.

Ⓘ Turn right. After 440 yards turn right again

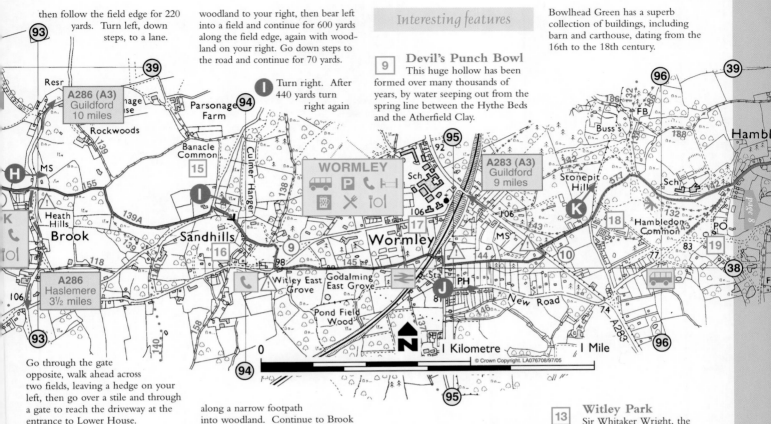

Interesting features

9 **Devil's Punch Bowl**
This huge hollow has been formed over many thousands of years, by water seeping out from the spring line between the Hythe Beds and the Atherfield Clay.

Bowlhead Green has a superb collection of buildings, including barn and carthouse, dating from the 16th to the 18th century.

Go through the gate opposite, walk ahead across two fields, leaving a hedge on your left, then go over a stile and through a gate to reach the driveway at the entrance to Lower House.

Ⓖ Go ahead through a tall kissing gate and down a field path into parkland. Cross a stile onto a sandy drive. Turn right. Follow a broad track up through parkland for 310 yards. Turn left immediately after a gateway. Go through a metal kissing gate. Bear right to follow a woodland path downhill to a kissing gate. Turn left onto the road and walk for 440 yards to the road (A286 Milford to Haslemere road), 330 yards to the north of Brook village.

Ⓗ Cross the road. Walk ahead up a track through woodland. After 400 yards, turn right at a triangle of grass. Follow the main footpath for 160 yards, leaving

along a narrow footpath into woodland. Continue to Brook Road. Cross this, then bear left along a broad track. Continue for 800 yards, over the railway and past Witley Station, to the road.

Ⓙ Cross the road and turn right. Turn left along a footpath opposite The Wood Pigeon. Turn left along the road (A283) for 30 yards, then turn right up a side road for 300 yards.

Ⓚ Bear left up a sandy track. After 380 yards bear right and continue uphill. At the top pass to the left of twin poles. Follow the footpath around the hilltop above Hambledon Common. Pass an old seat, then bear left down to the road at Hambledon.

10 **Hindhead Common**
Exmoor ponies and Highland cattle have been introduced to graze the slopes and maintain the heathland as it was created by grazing animals over 800 years ago.

11 **Church of St Michael and All Angels, Thursley**
In the churchyard you will find the stone erected in memory of the sailor murdered on Gibbet Hill. Eight chest tombs recall local 18th-century residents, more prosperous in their day than the sailor but less well remembered.

12 **Bowlhead Green**
A small hamlet between the parishes of Witley and Thursley,

13 **Witley Park**
Sir Whitaker Wright, the financier, restored Witley Park in the 1890s. At huge expense he included a glass-roofed room beneath the lake and six miles of walls round the grounds. The walls were considered the best in England.

14 **West Firs**
The unusual house on the hillside was built in 1960-1. Its design includes two wings, each based on a hexagon.

15 **Banacle Common**
Also known as Bannicle Hill, the Common served as one of the Admiralty Semaphore hills for a signalling system devised in 1816 and used between London and Portsmouth.

continued overleaf

16 Sandhills

The artists Miles Burkett Foster and Helen Allingham were among the intelligentsia who discovered Sandhills in the late 19th century and settled here.

17 Wormley

The station, opened here on 24 January 1859 was known as Witley for Chiddingfold until 1947. The village grew further from 1867, when King Edward's School was founded 'for 240 destitute children of both sexes'.

18 The Union Workhouse

The building which until recently housed part of The Royal Oceanographic Institute was built as The Union Workhouse in 1786 and later became The Hambledon Homes.

19 Oakhurst Cottage

The late 17th-century cottage, owned by the National Trust, survives as it was in the 19th century. It houses part of the Gertrude Jekyll collection of West Surrey Bygones.

Map 1c

Hambledon Common (SU 963384) ~ Gatestreet Farm (Grafham) (TQ 011419)
5 miles, allow 2½ hours

Route directions

A Turn left along Malthouse Lane. Go past Woodlands Road on the right and after 100 yards bear right up some steps behind cottages. Cross a stile and go ahead over fields, crossing two more stiles, to turn right to past Hambledon church.

B Bear right beyond the car park along a broad track. After 930 yards turn right by a bungalow. In 30 yards turn left up a narrow path.

C Walk beside the wood edge, then bear right downhill through woods along a broad path for 220 yards. Fork left and continue below the woods of Burgate Hangar for almost ½ mile to Markwick Lane.

D Turn left for 90 yards, then turn right, up a steeply-banked track. When you reach level ground continue along a broad track for just over ½ mile, ignoring all side tracks. When the path ahead begins a steep descent, turn right. Walk for 28 yards, then turn sharp left on a narrow footpath and go downhill. Cross a stile at the bottom then walk across fields, going over stiles and keeping to the right-hand side. Cross the road (B2130) to The White Horse Inn in Hascombe village. Walk up the side road, leaving the inn on your right.

E Follow the road past St Peter's Church and the pond. Bear left and continue to the road end. Go ahead through the gateway and walk up a drive. Go through a smaller gate onto a sandy track uphill. Once on the level go past a barn into woodland. Ignore a left fork and continue to cross tracks.

F Turn left along a broad path, then turn right after 300 yards down a deeply sunken path. Turn left at a T-junction to follow the track to the road. Turn right and walk along the road for 45 yards.

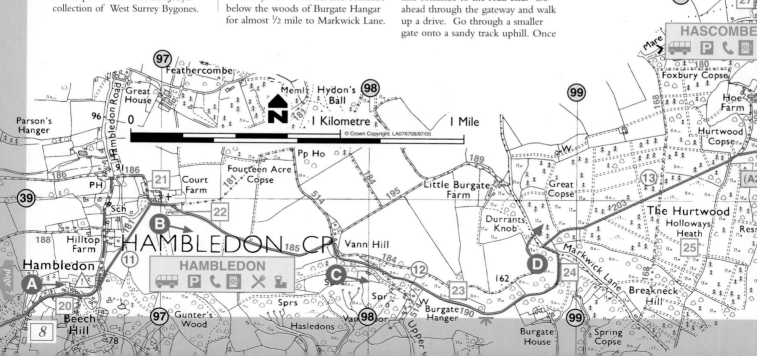

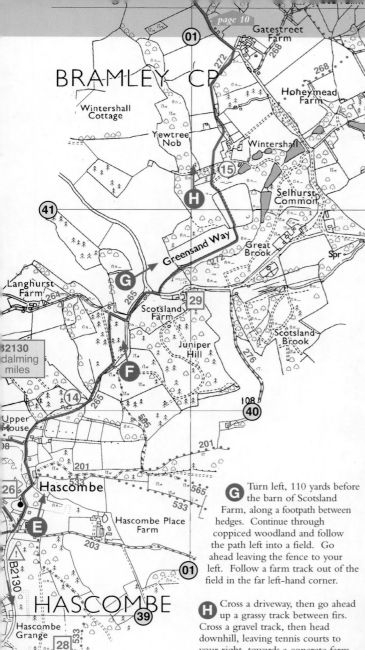

page 10

BRAMLEY CP

Wintershall Cottage

Yewtree Nob

Wintershall

Gatestreet Farm

Honeymead Farm

Selhurst Common

Greensand Way

Great Brook

Langhurst Farm

Scotsland Farm

Juniper Hill

Scotsland Brook

B2130 dalming miles

Upper House

Hascombe

Hascombe Place Farm

HASCOMBE

Hascombe Grange

Hascombe Hill

Interesting features

20 **Malthouse Lane, Hambledon**
In the process known as galleting, pieces of ironstone used to be inserted into the mortar in local houses. Said to keep the Devil away, it really saved mortar and added strength.

21 **Court Farm**
The farm was first built in the 17th century. The granary, also with hung-tiles, dates from the 18th century.

22 **Lime kiln**
The lime kiln, long disused, was first built in the 18th century. Before the lime kiln was constructed, local people used to dig marl from the ground to spread on the fields as fertiliser.

23 **Burgate Hangar**
The slopes of Burgate Hangar have been made steeper by land slips. They now provide a spectacular setting for hanging beeches.

24 **Markwick Lane**
Old lanes leading from the clay valley to the north, over the high ground of the Greensand ridge and

down to the Weald were frequently cut deeply into the sandstone of the Hythe Beds

25 **Holloways Heath**
Fallen trees still act as a reminder of the storm which felled an estimated 15 million trees in the early hours of 16 October 1987.

26 **St Peter's Church, Hascombe**
In this church, rebuilt by Henry Woodyer in 1864, the chancel roof is designed as an upturned fishing boat. A stained glass window depicting the patron saint continues the fishing theme.

27 **Hascombe village**
The village pond has served as both fish pond and millpond in its time. Shown on maps as marshy land at the beginning of the 20th century, it is now fully restored.

28 **Hascombe Hill**
Iron Age Celts built a fortified camp here towards the end of the first century BC. It had a single ditch and rampart across a narrow neck of land and just one entrance.

29 **Scotsland Farm**
The catslide roof of the 17th-century barn is one of the most prominent of its kind. Picturesquely named, the catslide provided an economic way of covering an extension used to house animals.

G Turn left, 110 yards before the barn of Scotsland Farm, along a footpath between hedges. Continue through coppiced woodland and follow the path left into a field. Go ahead leaving the fence to your left. Follow a farm track out of the field in the far left-hand corner.

H Cross a driveway, then go ahead up a grassy track between firs. Cross a gravel track, then head downhill, leaving tennis courts to your right, towards a concrete farm track by a right-hand fence. Turn left along the farm track, past farm buildings and continue along a broad track, with woods on your right, to Gatestreet. Turn left at the road.

Granary, Court Farm, Hambledon

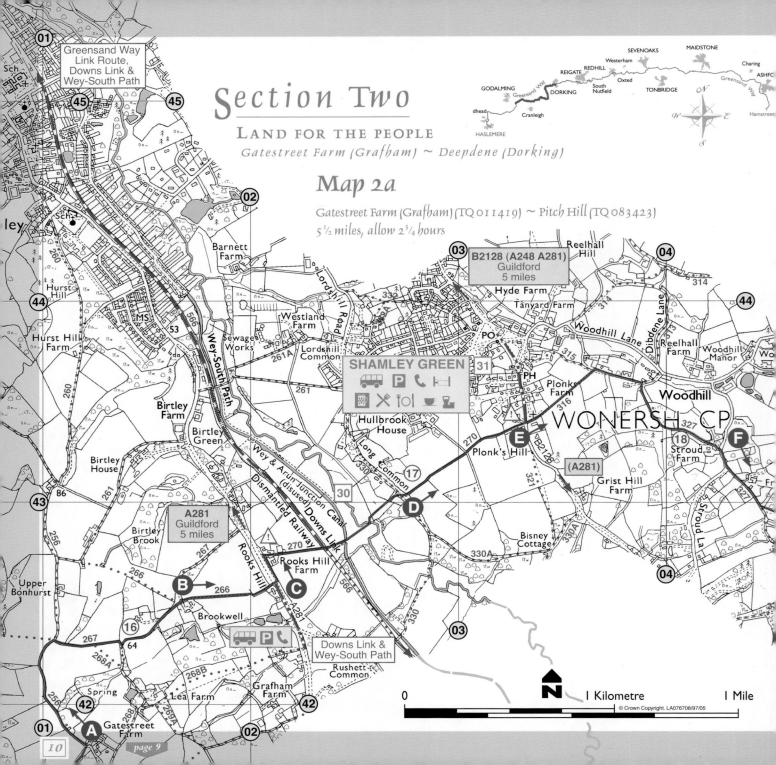

Section Two

LAND FOR THE PEOPLE

Gatestreet Farm (Grafham) ~ Deepdene (Dorking)

Map 2a

Gatestreet Farm (Grafham) (TQ 011419) ~ Pitch Hill (TQ 083423)
5½ miles, allow 2¾ hours

SEVENOAKS MAIDSTONE

WESTERHAM Charing ASHFC

REIGATE REDHILL Greensand Way

GODALMING DORKING South Nutfield Oxted TONBRIDGE Hamstreet

dhead Cranleigh HASLEMERE

Greensand Way Link Route, Downs Link & Wey-South Path

B2128 (A248 A281) Guildford 5 miles

Reelhall Hill

Hyde Farm

Tanyard Farm

Woodhill Lane

Dibdene Lane

Reelhall Farm

Woodhill Manor

PO

PH

SHAMLEY GREEN 31

Plonks Farm

Woodhill

WONERSH CP

Hullbrook House

Plonk's Hill

B2128

Stroud Farm

(A281)

Grist Hill Farm

Bisney Cottage

A281 Guildford 5 miles

Wey & Arun Junction Canal (disused) Downs Link

Dismantled Railway

Rooks Hill

Rooks Hill Farm

Birtley Brook

Upper Bonhurst

Brookwell

Downs Link & Wey-South Path

Rushett Common

Grafham Farm

Lea Farm

Spring

Gatestreet Farm

0   1 Kilometre   1 Mile

© Crown Copyright. LA076708/97/05

page 9

10

Route directions

A Turn left along a farm track. Then 275 yards past Keepers follow the lane to the right of a gate. Continue for 820 yards. Turn right, then left, to follow a metalled lane.

B Go ahead over the cattle grid beside Brookwell, then over a stile. Walk ahead along the field edge to a gate to the right of an oak tree. Continue between fences to the road (A281).

C Cross the road then turn left. Turn right through Rooks Hill Farm. Cross the old railway and the line of the disused canal. Go ahead through a gate to a footbridge. Walk up the slope, through gates. Bear right. Cross lane to a gate at Long Common.

D Go through the gate, then ahead between fields. Cross a farm track, then continue between fences to the road at Shamley Green.

E Cross the road and walk ahead to the right of the church.

Continue over stiles to a T-Junction. Turn right to a second T-Junction. Turn right and walk along the drive to Little Cucknells. Go downhill. At the house entrance keep ahead on the footpath, then continue over stiles, to the road at Stroud Farm.

F Turn right. After 100 yards bear left along the drive to Franklin's Farm. Follow the footpath to a stile. Cross into a field/garden. Bear left to the far corner. Cross a stile and walk uphill through a new plantation. Cross a stile then continue to a T-junction.

G Turn right. Walk generally uphill for 600 yards. Turn right at cross-tracks. Walk along a broad sandy path to the road. Bear left across the road and go up steps to a car park.

H Bear right from the far right-hand corner of the car park, then follow the track continuing as it narrows. Ignore all side paths. Pass a car park on the left and continue ahead. In 110 yards bear right. After 330 yards turn left. Cross a drive and

go ahead to the road. Turn right and go ahead alongside the road.

I Just beyond Jelley's Hollow bear right, then left and walk parallel to the road for 275 yards. Turn right to walk round Reynard's Hill. After 650 yards follow the main footpath down to Hurtwood Control Car Park (no 4). Turn right on the road and walk to a T-junction.

J Walk up the track opposite. Pass Ewhurst Cottage, then Ewhurst Windmill. Descend to the road and cross into Hurtwood Control Car Park (no 3). Turn right and follow the footpath uphill, past a quarry, for 490 yards to the top of Pitch Hill. Make for the toposcope.

Interesting features

30 Wey and Arun Canal The canal left the Wey Navigation at Shalford and rose 48 feet in six miles through seven locks

to Cranleigh before descending into West Sussex at Newbridge.

31 Shamley Green The name of Shamley may come from Shamble Lane, referring to the shelf of land on which the village lies.

32 Winterfold Heath The heath is part of the Hurtwood which takes its name from the hurts, or whortleberries, found there. Today it is part of a private estate where the public have the right of air and exercise .

33 Jelley's Hollow Traces of a possible Roman road have been found, running up the hollow towards Winterfold Heath. A road came from Stane Street and passed the site of a Roman temple at Farley Heath.

34 Ewhurst Windmill Probably the highest windmill in Surrey, this tower mill was first built in about 1840. Corn-milling ceased here around 1885.

Map 2b

Pitch Hill (TQ 083423) ~ Broadmoor (TQ 136457)
6 ½ miles, allow 3 ¼ hours

Route directions

(A) At the toposcope on Pitch Hill turn back through 45 degrees, then follow the path downhill along the hill edge. Pass a seat on your right then, after 65 yards, bear right down a narrow path.

(B) Turn left onto a metalled track. Go through a metal barrier, and continue along a broad track. Turn right after 330 yards. Follow the footpath downhill, then go down steps to the Duke of Kent School. Turn left along the drive.

(C) Cross the road and take the footpath ahead into woodland. Follow a fenced path up the slope to a stile, then continue to a metal gate. Bear right along

the lane for 65 yards, then turn sharp left, to follow a rough track uphill. Bear right to a road. Cross the road into the Hurtwood Control Car Park (no 1).

(D) Turn right to leave the car park and cross a gully. Go up steps and follow the footpath ahead uphill. After 710 yards cross the rampart of Holmbury Hill Fort. Make for the memorial seat on the summit then turn back through 45 degrees. Go ahead between wooden barriers and follow the footpath downhill, skirting the hillside. Swing left to merge with a broad track after 650 yards. Turn right at a junction of five tracks.

(E) Follow a broad path past a cricket pitch on your left. Turn left into Pitland Street. Bear right after 110 yards and continue to the main road (B2126 Abinger Hammer to Horsham road).

(F) Turn right, then first left. After 300 yards turn right up a sandy track and follow the path as it climbs uphill.

(G) Walk uphill to pass High Ashes Farm after 1 mile. Ignoring a downhill right-hand turn, continue to the T-junction.

(H) Turn right along a gravel track. Ignoring paths to left and right, continue to a T-junction. Turn left. Bear right across the road. Go ahead up a broad track to reach Leith Hill Tower after 980 yards. Walk ahead past the tower, going downhill, for 220 yards.

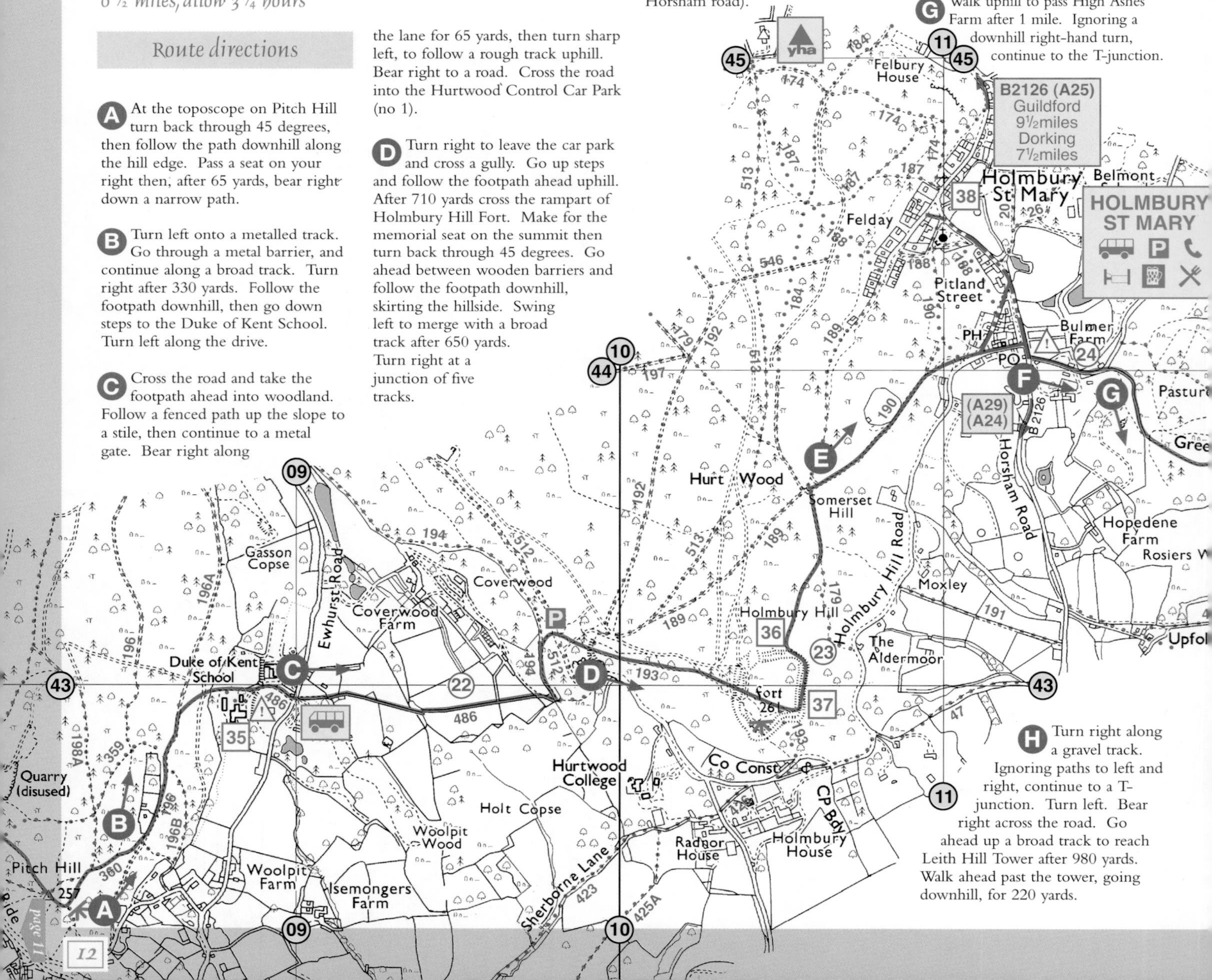

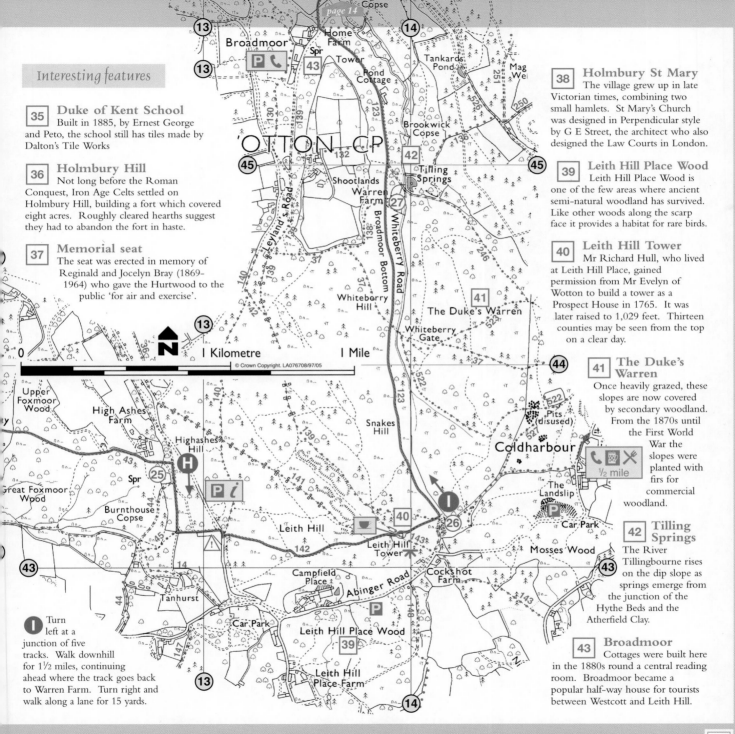

Interesting features

35 Duke of Kent School
Built in 1885, by Ernest George and Peto, the school still has tiles made by Dalton's Tile Works

36 Holmbury Hill
Not long before the Roman Conquest, Iron Age Celts settled on Holmbury Hill, building a fort which covered eight acres. Roughly cleared hearths suggest they had to abandon the fort in haste.

37 Memorial seat
The seat was erected in memory of Reginald and Jocelyn Bray (1869–1964) who gave the Hurtwood to the public 'for air and exercise'.

38 Holmbury St Mary
The village grew up in late Victorian times, combining two small hamlets. St Mary's Church was designed in Perpendicular style by G E Street, the architect who also designed the Law Courts in London.

39 Leith Hill Place Wood
Leith Hill Place Wood is one of the few areas where ancient semi-natural woodland has survived. Like other woods along the scarp face it provides a habitat for rare birds.

40 Leith Hill Tower
Mr Richard Hull, who lived at Leith Hill Place, gained permission from Mr Evelyn of Wotton to build a tower as a Prospect House in 1765. It was later raised to 1,029 feet. Thirteen counties may be seen from the top on a clear day.

41 The Duke's Warren
Once heavily grazed, these slopes are now covered by secondary woodland. From the 1870s until the First World War the slopes were planted with firs for commercial woodland.

42 Tilling Springs
The River Tillingbourne rises on the dip slope as springs emerge from the junction of the Hythe Beds and the Atherfield Clay.

43 Broadmoor
Cottages were built here in the 1880s round a central reading room. Broadmoor became a popular half-way house for tourists between Westcott and Leith Hill.

I Turn left at a junction of five tracks. Walk downhill for 1½ miles, continuing ahead where the track goes back to Warren Farm. Turn right and walk along a lane for 15 yards.

0   1 Kilometre   1 Mile

© Crown Copyright. LA076708/97/05

Map 2c

Broadmoor (TQ 136457) ~
Deepdene (Dorking) (TQ 175491)
5½ miles, allow 2¾ hours

Route directions

WESTCOTT

WOTTON

A Bear right along a track. Cross the River Tillingbourne and walk down the right side of the valley, following the main track for one mile to a private drive.

B Bear right along the drive for 35 yards. Turn right onto the road, then, almost immediately, turn sharp right along a footpath beside a cinder track. Bear right at the junction of tracks, then turn left under a beech tree and follow a footpath, going downhill through woodland. Bear right after 490 yards and continue to pass the entrance pillars to Rookery Drive at Westcott.

C Turn right along a sandy path and continue uphill past a quarry. At a T-junction keep ahead on the footpath. Bear left across a lane and continue along Westcott Heath, running parallel with the lane. Cross a lane which leads left downhill to Holy Trinity Church. Continue ahead through more woodland to Heath Rise, just above The Cricketers.

D Cross Heath Rise. Continue ahead along a footpath behind gardens. Go through a barrier and across a metalled parking area behind houses. Continue along a hedged path, then pass a field entrance and continue downhill.

E Cross a footbridge over a stream. Turn left, then turn right after 90 yards and go up steps. Go through a gate and turn left along a metalled track. Walk along the lane for 330 yards.

F Turn right through a small clearing in

A25 Guildford 9 miles

Greensand Way Link Route

North Downs Way

Greensand Way Link Route

woodland. Bear right where the path forks after 45 yards. Continue uphill through trees to reach The Temple at the top of The Nower. Continue ahead past The Temple for 550 yards.

G Turn left at a seat and go down the slope to the far right-hand corner of a field. At the end of beech hedging turn right between hedges. Go to the left of a gate and cross Hampstead Lane. Turn right, then left along Nower Road. Continue for 165 yards.

H Turn right by a post box and walk ahead to continue along a footpath leading down-hill. Go through barriers onto the pavement by Vincent Lane (A25/A2003 in town one-way system). Turn left to the end of the barrier, then cross the road. Turn right and pass the telephone box on the corner beside a garage. Cross the road at the pedestrian crossing just after the bend. Turn left. Cross road (A2003), using the central reservation, and go up a narrow path to the right of The Queen's Head.

I Go between barriers at the top. Turn right along Peacock Walk, then turn left between barriers into St Paul's Road. Where the road bears right, uphill, into South Terrace, go ahead along St Paul's Road West.

J Turn right just before St Paul's C of E School. Go through a gate and continue ahead uphill. Go through another gate into The Glory Wood. Follow the path left, then right, uphill. Turn left at a T-junction. Continue on the path through the woods, above the field edge, then bear left and walk down to join the road.

K Turn right at Chart Lane to reach the main road (A24). Cross Deepdene Avenue, using the central reservation. Turn left along the road for 10 yards, then turn sharp right, uphill. Where the main track bears right, turn left, and go up steps. Follow a broad track to a horse barrier. Turn left onto a metalled track by Deepdene End.

Interesting features

44 Tillingbourne Falls
A Dutch merchant named Jacobson built the ornamental waterfall around 1740 as part of the Evelyns' garden landscape scheme. It took its head of water from ponds at a mill upstream at Brookmill

45 Wolven's Lane
The name means 'foul or muddy fen' referring to the damp slopes. Smugglers used this ancient road in the 18th and early 19th century to bring contraband to London from the south coast

46 River Tillingbourne
The River Tillingbourne rises from springs at the junction of the Hythe Beds and the Atherfield Clay on the dip slope of the Lower Greensand.

47 Pipp Brook
This important tributary of the River Mole flows through Dorking. At one time it supported in its five-mile length seven watermills and one water-pumping mill, including Pixham Mill, at Dorking.

48 The Rookery
In 1759, David Malthus, father of Thomas Malthus, the economist, bought the Rookery estate. The two ornamental lakes were part of his landscaping. Before that two watermills stood on the stream.

49 Holy Trinity Church, Westcott
Known as Westcote in Domesday Book, at the west end of the parish of Dorking, Westcott only acquired its own church in 1851-2 on land given by the Evelyn family. Sir George Gilbert-Scott designed it in 14th-century style.

50 The Nower
The Nower belonged to Osbert del Ore in 1247. Its modern name first appeared when it was owned by Thomas ate Nore in the 14th century.

51 The Temple
The Temple and its seat were built early in the 20th century by the Barclay family, who gave The Nower to Dorking in 1931.

52 Dorking
Dorking became a market centre for outlying districts as early as Saxon times. In medieval times timber from the local hillsides was transported through Dorking for use in London and other larger towns.

53 St Martin's Church, Dorking (TQ 165495)
St Martin's Church was built between 1868 and 1877 following a design by Henry Woodyer, in late-Gothic style.

54 Tumulus
A bowl barrow found here was used by people from late Stone Age to Bronze Age times, from between 2400 and 1500 BC.

55 The Glory Wood
In the mid-19th century a group of firs, known as The Glory, stood out on the hilltop. Beech trees began to cover the slopes later in the century.

56 Deepdene House
From the 17th century, successive owners built houses or added wings to a palatial house here, renowned for its stylish design.

57 Box Hill (TQ 180512)
Named after the evergreen box tree which grows on its slopes above the River Mole, Box Hill offers a mixture of habitats, some mature woodland, some open chalk downland. In winter sheep graze its thousand acres to help to conserve the plant life.

Section Three

INDUSTRY PAST AND PRESENT
Deepdene (Dorking) ~ Oxted Place

Map 3a

Deepdene (Dorking) (TQ 175491) ~ Reigate Park (TQ 247494)
6 miles, allow 3 hours

Route directions

A Turn left onto a metalled track by Deepdene End. Turn right at the T-Junction, then right again along Punchbowl Lane. Turn left at the entrance to Park Farm.

B Go ahead to pass farm buildings. Go under the railway bridge, and continue beside the old hedgeline. At the end of the field turn right, then immediately left, and cross a stile. Go ahead along the field edge and through a gate, then continue to the next field corner. Cross the stile. Turn left to another stile by Pondtail Farm.

C Cross a farm road, then continue ahead over three stiles. Turn right along a sandy farm track. Turn left at the end, along the road to Brockham Village Green. Cross this, then bear right to cross the Green along the road passing The Duke's Head and The Royal Oak. Continue to a wooden gate at the end of the road.

D Turn left along a metalled path. Cross the bridge over the River Mole, and bear right along the path above the river. Go past houses and cross a bridge. Continue ahead beside fields for 770 yards. Go ahead through gates beside a farm. Cross a driveway and take the path through the churchyard to the right of the Church of St Michael and All Angels, Betchworth. Go through the stone gateway and ahead past Forge Cottage.

E Cross the road and go ahead along Wonham Lane. Walk for 100 yards, then bear left along a gravel footpath. Continue parallel with the road, then bear left into a field and follow the hedge on your right to the near right-hand corner of the field

F Turn left along Sandy Lane and walk up to a T-junction. Turn right, then, in 55 yards, turn right again, up steps and continue to a stile. Cross the stile and continue ahead. After 165 yards, bear left across the field to a gate and stile in the far left-hand corner. Cross the stile, then turn right and almost immediately cross the stile on the far side of the lane.

G Go ahead, with the hedge on your left, to a metal kissing gate. Continue ahead, now with a hedge on your right, to another kissing gate and follow a small path to the

road. Turn right down a farm lane (Dungates Lane). Turn left through Dungate's farmyard with farm buildings either side. Walk for 1/4 mile to a Y-junction.

H Bear right through a double gate. Follow a broad track diagonally across a field. Go through a gate and continue along a track to pass Ivy Cottage. Turn left at cross tracks then right almost immediately to follow the footpath across Reigate Heath Golf Course. Go up the track to the windmill. Pass the windmill on your left, ignoring two small tracks to the right.

I Turn sharp right down a footpath just before the main

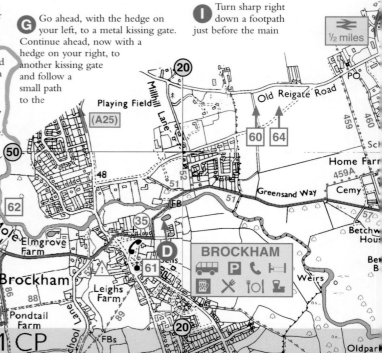

track bends left. Continue across Flanchford Road and follow the metalled track past The White House. Bear right uphill into woodland, past Ivy Cottage. Go ahead down a narrow track. Continue past The Skimmington Castle and walk down the slope ahead to a cross track.

J Turn right along the track and follow this to reach the road after 330 yards. Continue ahead along the road, (Littleton Lane), bearing left then climbing uphill for 600 yards to a T-junction. Cross the road and go up steps to Reigate Park.

Interesting features

58 Park Farm
First built in the 1550s, this farm became the home farm for Deepdene. The red brick and tiles cover timber framing.

59 Betchworth Park
In the Middle Ages a castle stood beside the River Mole, to the north of Betchworth Park. The park was later renowned for its chestnuts and its elm avenues.

60 Quarries (TQ206516)
Chalk pits and lime works produced hearthstone and firestone as well as lime for agricultural use. The works were known for the Brockham

continued overleaf

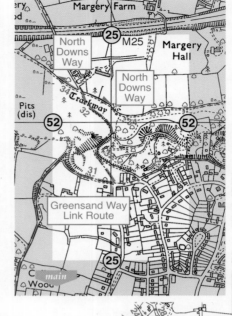

0   1 Kilometre   1 Mile

© Crown Copyright. LA076708/97/05

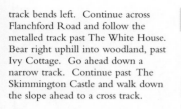

BETCHWORTH

continued from previous page

Continuous Lime Kiln patented there in 1889. Bricks were produced into the 20th century

61 Christchurch, Brockham
Designed by Benjamin Ferrey, a pupil of the architect Pugin, and completed in 1846, this church was built from carefully selected stone from the quarries at Betchworth. Before it was built villagers went to church in Betchworth.

62 River Mole.
Some say the river takes its name from the animal since, on occasions during drought, it flows underground between Dorking and Leatherhead. Others claim that the Latin Mola for Mill is more apt in view of the many watermills the river powered.

63 Betchworth village
The name of The Dolphin Inn is thought to have come from the French Dauphin who may have passed this way.

64 Old Industry
(TQ 206516)
The Dorking Greystone Lime Company, who also took over the Brockham works, operated the chalk pits and lime works between 1865 and 1934.

65 Dungate's Farm
The house and barn have stood here since the late 16th century. Stephen Dungate of Betchworth is recorded as the owner in 1731.

66 Reigate Heath
Long barrows on the north of the Heath reveal a Neolithic burial site. Settlers in the region may have traded between Stonehenge and the Low Countries.

67 Reigate Heath Mill
A post mill was built here around 1765. The mill ceased working in about 1870 and was converted to a chapel of ease to St Mary's Parish Church, Reigate, in 1880.

View over Reigate Heath, looking towards old quarries and North Downs from the slopes of Reigate Park

Map 3b

Reigate Park (TQ247494) ~ *Castle Hill* (TQ 320505)
7 miles, allow 3½ hours

68 Reigate Park
A memorial commemorates Mr and Mrs Randall Vogen's gift of the park to the corporation in 1920.

69 Reigate Priory
A priory was founded here in the 13th century for Augustinian canons. After the Dissolution of the Monasteries Lord William Howard converted the buildings into a Tudor mansion.

70 Reigate
After the castle was built in 1088, a town grew up known as Reigate, 'the gap through which Roe Deer were hunted'. The town replaced the earlier village of Cherchefelle for which St Mary's Church was first built.

71 Redhill
The low-lying land, once the preserve of farms and tiny hamlets, was transformed into a residential area by the arrival of the railway, the London, Brighton and South Coast Railway in 1841 and the South-Eastern Railway between 1842 and 1849

72 Redhill Common
St John's Church was built in 1843 on the lower slopes of Redhill Common to provide for the increasing population.

Entrance to Reigate Castle

73 Earlswood Common
Held by the first Earls of Surrey, this was part of the wastes of the manor of Reigate and remained common land until the 19th century.

74 Nutfield Priory
Prominent on the hillside, Nutfield Priory looks like a Tudor building. It was built in 1872 by the architect, John Gibson, as a private house in a style favoured at the time.

75 Redhill Aerodrome (TQ 301477)
The aerodrome was established in 1934 and used to train Imperial Airways engineers. The Redhill Flying Club and an RAF training school were formed in 1937.

76 King's Mill
A brick and weather-boarded corn mill with a mansard roof, this mill first appears on a map of 1768. It continued to be run, with water power until 1944, then by electricity until 1963.

77 Nutfield
The area has long been known for its resources of fuller's earth, much of which is now exhausted. A nature reserve has been created on the site of old processing plants

78 South Nutfield Railway
Designed by Sir William Cubitt who is said to have taken sightings from the view-point on Redhill Common, it is noted for the straightness of its line.

continued overleaf

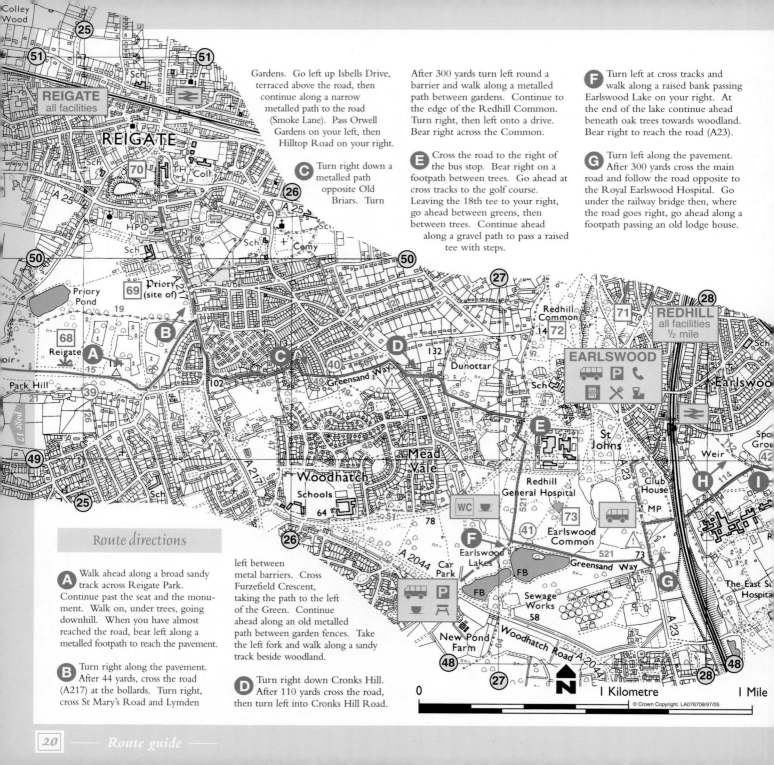

Gardens. Go left up Isbells Drive, terraced above the road, then continue along a narrow metalled path to the road (Smoke Lane). Pass Orwell Gardens on your left, then Hilltop Road on your right.

C Turn right down a metalled path opposite Old Briars. Turn

After 300 yards turn left round a barrier and walk along a metalled path between gardens. Continue to the edge of the Redhill Common. Turn right, then left onto a drive. Bear right across the Common.

E Cross the road to the right of the bus stop. Bear right on a footpath between trees. Go ahead at cross tracks to the golf course. Leaving the 18th tee to your right, go ahead between greens, then between trees. Continue ahead along a gravel path to pass a raised tee with steps.

F Turn left at cross tracks and walk along a raised bank passing Earlswood Lake on your right. At the end of the lake continue ahead beneath oak trees towards woodland. Bear right to reach the road (A23).

G Turn left along the pavement. After 300 yards cross the main road and follow the road opposite to the Royal Earlswood Hospital. Go under the railway bridge then, where the road goes right, go ahead along a footpath passing an old lodge house.

Route directions

A Walk ahead along a broad sandy track across Reigate Park. Continue past the seat and the monument. Walk on, under trees, going downhill. When you have almost reached the road, bear left along a metalled footpath to reach the pavement.

B Turn right along the pavement. After 44 yards, cross the road (A217) at the bollards. Turn right, cross St Mary's Road and Lymden

left between metal barriers. Cross Furzefield Crescent, taking the path to the left of the Green. Continue ahead along an old metalled path between garden fences. Take the left fork and walk along a sandy track beside woodland.

D Turn right down Cronks Hill. After 110 yards cross the road, then turn left into Cronks Hill Road.

0   1 Kilometre   1 Mile

© Crown Copyright. LA076708/97/05

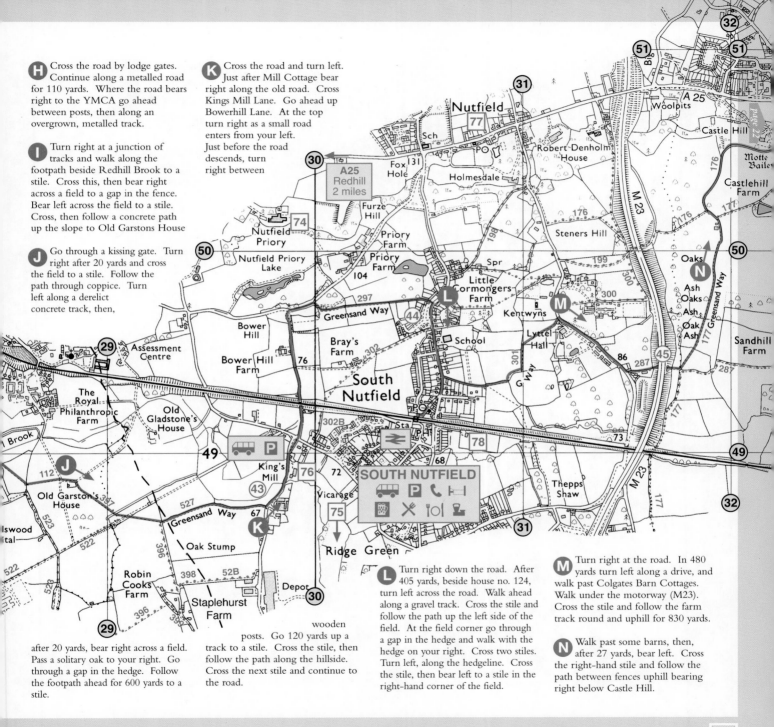

H Cross the road by lodge gates. Continue along a metalled road for 110 yards. Where the road bears right to the YMCA go ahead between posts, then along an overgrown, metalled track.

I Turn right at a junction of tracks and walk along the footpath beside Redhill Brook to a stile. Cross this, then bear right across a field to a gap in the fence. Bear left across the field to a stile. Cross, then follow a concrete path up the slope to Old Garstons House

J Go through a kissing gate. Turn right after 20 yards and cross the field to a stile. Follow the path through coppice. Turn left along a derelict concrete track, then,

K Cross the road and turn left. Just after Mill Cottage bear right along the old road. Cross Kings Mill Lane. Go ahead up Bowerhill Lane. At the top turn right as a small road enters from your left. Just before the road descends, turn right between

after 20 yards, bear right across a field. Pass a solitary oak to your right. Go through a gap in the hedge. Follow the footpath ahead for 600 yards to a stile.

wooden posts. Go 120 yards up a track to a stile. Cross the stile, then follow the path along the hillside. Cross the next stile and continue to the road.

L Turn right down the road. After 405 yards, beside house no. 124, turn left across the road. Walk ahead along a gravel track. Cross the stile and follow the path up the left side of the field. At the field corner go through a gap in the hedge and walk with the hedge on your right. Cross two stiles. Turn left, along the hedgeline. Cross the stile, then bear left to a stile in the right-hand corner of the field.

M Turn right at the road. In 480 yards turn left along a drive, and walk past Colgates Barn Cottages. Walk under the motorway (M23). Cross the stile and follow the farm track round and uphill for 830 yards.

N Walk past some barns, then, after 27 yards, bear left. Cross the right-hand stile and follow the path between fences uphill bearing right below Castle Hill.

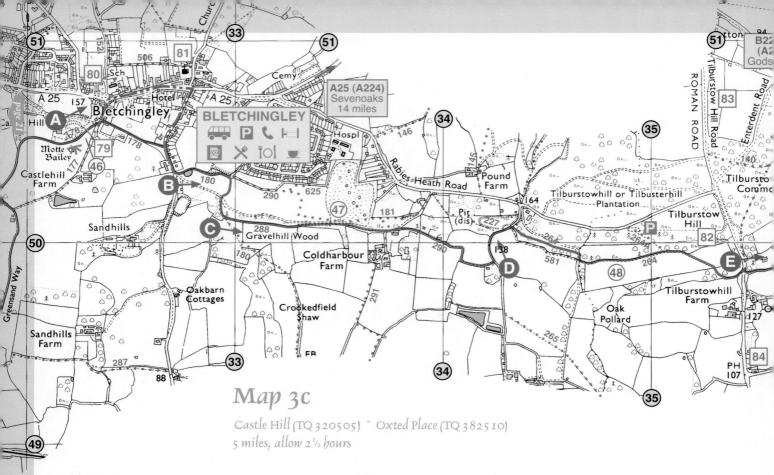

Map 3c

Castle Hill (TQ 320505) ~ Oxted Place (TQ 382510)

5 miles, allow 2½ hours

Route directions

A Walk beneath a steep embankment and continue to the road. Cross the road and follow the footpath ahead to steps leading down to another road. Turn right. In 175 yards turn left at the entrance to a now-disused quarry.

B In 22 yards turn left down a track beside a metal gate. Follow the gravel track leaving a pond to your right. In 275 yards turn right along a fenced path to go through old workings. Cross a concrete road and follow the track

ahead, ignoring side tracks. Bear left with the track and continue to the road.

C Follow the road for a thousand yards. Where the road bends left at a green triangle follow the track ahead. Walk past houses along a gravelled track, then continue along a field path for 380 yards to a road.

D Turn left. After 350 yards turn right along a bridleway and follow through woods to cross-tracks. Turn right and then left to follow the path below the hill, to reach the road after a thousand yards.

E Bear right across the road and continue along a broad track below Brakey Hill for 820 yards, ignoring all turnings to the right until 10 yards before a gate across the track. Here turn right over a stile. Walk ahead for 300 yards across the field, then bear left towards the top far left-hand corner. Cross a stile and follow the path ahead to the road (B2236).

F Cross the road and turn left. Walk for 330 yards to a triangle where the main road bends left. Here turn right to pass Leigh Mill House on your left. Cross a foot-, bridge beside a ford and after 330

yards continue ahead through a kissing gate to the Godstone by-pass (A22).

G Cross the by-pass and go through a kissing gate ahead. Follow the path ahead for 950 yards to the road at Tandridge. Cross the road and turn right. Turn left after 80 yards and continue along a path to the right of The Barley Mow.

H Follow the path round to the left, then bear right up a narrow path to the right of garages. Cross a stile and walk along the top of a field to a kissing gate in the far left-hand corner. Bear right and follow the path ahead.

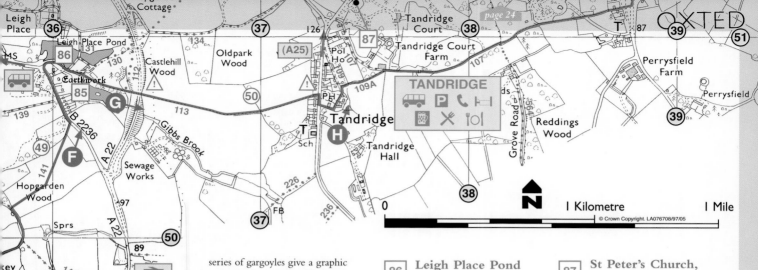

page 24

Interesting features

series of gargoyles give a graphic account of vice and madness.

82 Tilburstow Hill
Once the place of Tilbeorht's Tree, the name of this hill has undergone almost as many changes as the valuable woodland which now covers it.

83 Tilburstow Hill Road
Carriers who took iron and charcoal from the Weald up this old Roman road were required to carry loads of stone to mend the road as they damaged it.

84 Fox and Hounds Inn
This 16th-century building with fish-scale tile-hanging on the upper storey was well placed as an Ale House to give people respite before the long pull uphill.

85 Leigh Mill, Godstone
Recorded as a corn mill in Domesday Book, abandoned at the time of the Black Death, then used for gunpowder manufacture in the 17th century, the present brick and weather-boarded building dates from the 18th century.

86 Leigh Place Pond
Now an SSSI, this pond was first created when the Evelyn brothers dammed the Gibb Brook to maintain a steady water supply for the wheel at Leigh Mill gunpowder works.

87 St Peter's Church, Tandridge
A huge yew tree, said to be the oldest and largest in Britain, stands outside the church whose shingled bell tower has stood since around 1300 AD.

79 Bletchingley Castle
The de Clare family who were also Lords of Tonbridge built a solid castle here. It was demolished in 1264 during the war between Simon de Montfort and Henry III.

80 Bletchingley
(formerly Blechingley)
The medieval market took place at the east end of the village near St Mary's Church. The Whyte Horse Inn has stood there since 1388.

81 St Mary's Church, Bletchingley
This impressive church has a Norman tower and Perpendicular chapel, arcades and chancel arch. A

Cottage with hung tiles, Bletchingly

Section Four

THE GROWTH OF THE COUNTRY HOUSE

Oxted Place ~ Shipbourne Common

Route directions

A Continue along a metalled track at the entrance to The Mount. Cross the drive and continue to the road at Broadham Green. Turn left along the road, then right along Tanhouse Road. Turn left and cross a stile opposite The Hay Cutter. Walk along the right-hand side of the field to a stile. Cross, then bear left and follow the path over the stile to a complex of buildings at Oxted Mill.

B Continue to the road. Turn right along the road and walk uphill to Woodhurst Lane. Cross, then turn left. After 22 yards turn right up a narrow path. Walk for 400 yards between gardens, then along a metalled drive to a T-junction.

OXTED all facilities

OLD OXTED

LIMPSFIELD

BROADHAM GREEN

Greensand Way Link Route

A25 Redhill 7½ miles

A25 (A224) Sevenoaks 8½ miles

Limpsfield Common

West Heath

Mill Barn

Stonehall Farm

Tanhouse Farm

Oxted Place

Broadham Green

Oxted Mill

Beechwood Hill

Tandridge Court

Chalkpit Wood

Limpsfield Grange Sch

Neolithic Implements found

Vanguard Way

North Downs Way

Quarry Works

North Downs Way

OXTED CP

Golf Course

1 Kilometre

© Crown Copyright. LA076708/97/05

24 page 23

Map 4a

Oxted Place (TQ 382510) ~ Mariners Hill (TQ 451516)

5½ miles, allow 2¾ hours

C Turn left along the road. After 220 yards cross the road and follow the track ahead to Limpsfield Common. Bear right then immediately left along a metalled lane with Limpsfield Common on your right. At St Michael's School, turn right across the road and walk over the Common to another road.

D Cross the road. Go ahead through a car park, then follow the main track left then right over the Common to another road. Bear

right along the road, then, after 120 yards, bear left onto a footpath across the golf course.

E Cross the road. Go over the stile to the left of Pains Hill Chapel and follow the path to the road. Turn left and walk to the end of the road. Turn left along a gravel lane at Pastons Cottage, and continue along the footpath ahead to the road at Limpsfield Chart.

continued overleaf

continued overleaf

continued from previous page

F Cross the road, turn right and walk along the tarmac path for 185 yards. Bear left along a path. Cross the road and go ahead, along an unmade road, then a footpath to a road. Bear left, pass The Carpenter's Arms and follow footway to a T-junction.

G Cross and follow the path ahead, then bear left. Follow a path for about 2/3 mile, going over two broad cross-tracks. Bear left at a junction and continue to a meeting of six tracks at the County boundary. Take the track ahead between houses to the road at Goodley Stock. Cross the road to a stile. Walk across a clearing to a track.

H Turn right downhill through woodland to a stile. Cross the stile, then turn left just before the

road at a small clearing. Walk uphill for 220 yards. Turn right and walk for 275 yards, then bear left at a junction of seven tracks.

I After 380 yards, go over a broad cross track to a seat and bear left past it, leaving The Warren to your right. Continue ahead, to go downhill through woodland. Turn right after 380 yards towards the road. Turn left along the road, then almost immediately bear right to follow a stony track uphill. After 110 yards take the left fork and walk across Mariners Hill.

Interesting features

88 **Oxted Mill**
A water mill has stood here since the mid-19th century, with an extension built in 1893. This was

powered by a turbine and produced much finer flour, than before.

89 **Old Oxted**
This settlement mainly lies along one street and contains timber-framed buildings from the 16th century. The Old Bell at the crossroads has an interesting jettied upper floor.

90 **Former St Michael's School for Girls**
The Gothic tower of this red-brick building, built in 1886, provides a landmark for miles around.

91 **Limpsfield Common**
When the Lord of the Manor first tried to establish brickworks here in 1830 he caused uproar among the Commoners who had held rights since the 14th century.

92 **The Salt Box**
This 16th-century house may have been used for the drying of salt

brought from the south coast on its way to London.

93 **Squerryes Court**
The fine, red-brick manor house was built in the time of William and Mary. In the garden James Wolfe was commissioned into the Army as a boy of 14 in 1741.

94 **St Mary's Church**
The squat, shingled spire rises above a 13th-century church. Inside, the Royal Arms of Edward VI are the earliest example of this particular coat of arms to be found in England.

95 **Quebec House, Westerham**
Sir James Wolfe spent his early years in this gabled, red-bricked house. The house was renamed after the Battle of Quebec where Wolfe died of wounds after winning the battle.

Squerries Court

Map 4b

Mariners Hill (TQ 451516) ~ Dale Farm (TQ 524513)
6¼ miles, allow 3 hours

Interesting features

96 **Chartwell**
Sir Winston Churchill bought this house in 1922 and made it his family home. Much of the house, now owned by the National Trust, is on view, furnished as it was in his and Lady Churchill's lifetime.

97 **French Street**
In 1927 workers digging for gravel found a hoard of coins dating from the Iron Age. Known as the Westerham Gold, these 14 gold staters had been hidden by Celtic people.

98 **Toys Hill**
At 801 feet and the highest point in Kent, Toys Hill suffered severe damage in the storm of 1987. Ten years on the woodland has again concealed the views that were revealed at the time.

99 **Emmetts**
The six-acre garden, the highest garden in Kent, contains many fine shrubs, including azaleas and rhododendrons.

100 **St Mary's Church, Ide Hill**
Built in 1865 at a cost of £2,805, the small church today contains a chancel ceiling dedicated to the memory of President Kennedy.

101 **Hanging Bank**
This area of the Greensand ridge is noted for its landslips. A fall here in 1929 created this particularly steep section.

102 **Bough Beech Reservoir** (TQ 95482)
The reservoir was created by enlarging part of the River Eden. It provides a centre for sailing boats and is an important wildlife habitat.

103 **Wickhurst Manor**
Rebuilt in the 19th century, the house still contains some of its original structure as a Wealden hall house. A 15th-century doorway has been preserved in the south wall.

Route directions

A Continue over Mariners Hill to the road at Chartwell. Cross the road to a stile to the left of the house entrance. Go ahead up the path. At the top cross a road and follow the track ahead to the right of the gate. Continue on the track above the combe for 550 yards, then follow the metalled path to the junction with the road.

B Turn right and go downhill to Frenchstreet Farm. Continue along a broad lane along the centre of the valley. Where the lane turns left to Highview Cottage, go ahead taking the bridleway to Toys Hill. After 260 yards bear left to follow a sandy lane beside Frenchstreet Nurseries. Continue for 440 yards to a T-junction where turn sharp right. At cross tracks in a clearing turn left uphill. Take the steps down to the car park on Toys Hill and bear right to the road.

continued overleaf

Toys Hill

continued from previous page

C Cross the road and follow the track ahead to a clearing where five tracks meet. Go ahead downhill to a stile. Cross into a field, turn left along the headland then continue to a stile. Cross this, then walk downhill to the far right-hand corner of the field

D Cross a bridge over a stream and continue up the left side of the field to a stile beside a gate. Cross, then continue ahead uphill to join a broad farm track leading uphill.

Go over a last stile at the top and walk ahead along a metalled track to Ide Hill village.

E Turn right towards the Green. Turn right just past Glebe House along a metalled footpath. Bear right along a gravelled path, then fork left down a grassy track. Turn left and follow the path round the hillside above the road. Follow the path down to the road.

F Cross the road to go along roadside edge of the car park. Where the road swings left uphill bear right along a metalled track.

G Fork left almost immediately and continue along a bridleway then turn back sharp left and go uphill. Turn right after 110 yards and follow the path with a post and rail fence on your right. Bear left downhill at cross tracks, then turn right uphill to the car park at Goathurst Common.

H Cross the road, then follow the path ahead to a small car park. Continue ahead for 220 yards. Turn right down steps on footpath 203. Cross a stile and walk along the top of a field below woods to another stile. Cross, then follow the path across a broad field, going past a pond to a disused stile. Bear right and continue to a stile in the fence.

I Cross into woodland, then bear left to a stile at the edge of the wood. Cross, then bear right and walk across fields to a gate by woodland. Continue beside the wood towards a farm. Just before a pond turn left over a small bridge. Cross a stile and turn right. Go ahead to the far right-hand corner of the field, then turn right over a stile to the right of a gate.

J Turn left along road for 165 yards. Turn right at the next gate and go down the side of the field, leaving the hedge and a line of oaks on your left. Where the ground levels out head across the field towards the right-hand side of a farm, over stile and along concrete

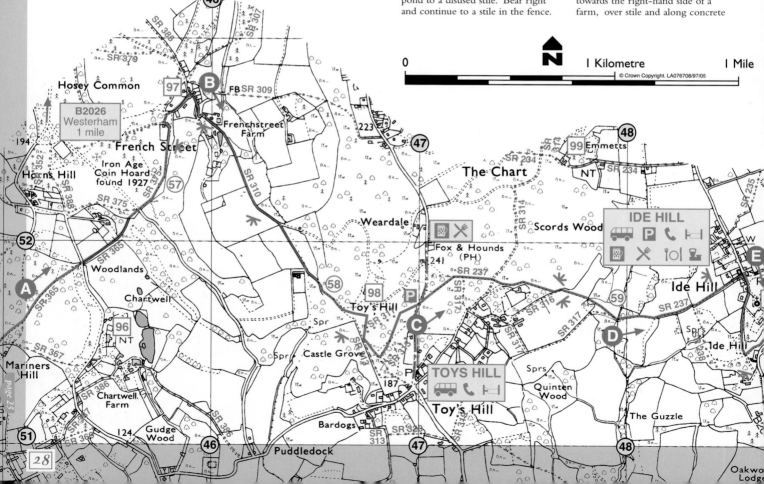

farm path. Pass Wickhurst Manor and Wickhurst Manor Farm.

K Turn left following footpath 264, then immediately right over a stile. Go uphill along footpath 268 to a stile at the top of the slope. Continue across a field to a stile to the left of farm buildings. Walk past the farm buildings to a stile then bear right over a field to a marker set in front of trees on the far side. Walk between coppiced beeches. Cross a stile, go over a stream, then go through the hedge line towards the oast of Dale Farm.

Map 4c *(map overleaf)*

Dale Farm (TQ 524513) ~ Shipbourne Common (TQ 597523)

6 ¼ miles, allow 3 hours

Interesting features

104 **St George's Church, Sevenoaks Weald**
Outside, this church, first built in 1820 of Portland rather than local stone, looks severe. Inside there is rich late-Victorian stencilling in the chancel of 1872.

105 **Long Barn** (TQ 526506)
In a Dutch garden designed by Lutyens, Harold Nicolson and Vita Sackville-West created their first garden before moving on to Sissinghurst.

106 **Hubbard's Hill**
The curiously curved mounds below Hubbards Hill were formed by debris left when thawed soil from higher up the hill slipped downwards over frozen ground.

107 **Riverhill**
John Rogers, an early member of the Royal Horticultural Society, established a garden here with newly imported plants on the acid, Wealden soil. Cedars of Lebanon and a Wellingtonia flourish as well as azaleas and rhododendrons.

108 **Knole**
First built by Thomas Bourchier, Archbishop of Canterbury between 1456 and 1486, and enlarged by Henry VIII, this important Tudor mansion became the home of the Sackvilles.

109 **Knole Park**
The thousand acre park provides important wildlife habitats. Dead wood from the trees supports rare fungus and lichen and also sustains the finest invertebrate collection in Kent.

110 **Sevenoaks**
The town's name can be traced to the 12th century when it was known as Seovenaca. Six of the well-known seven oaks came down in the storm of 1987. They had been planted in 1902 to commemorate the coronation of Edward VII.

continued overleaf

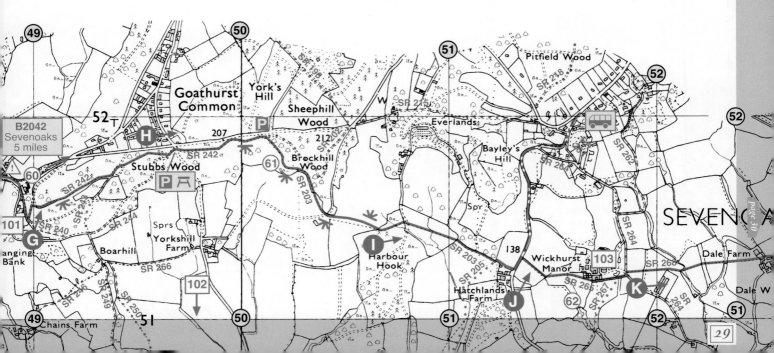

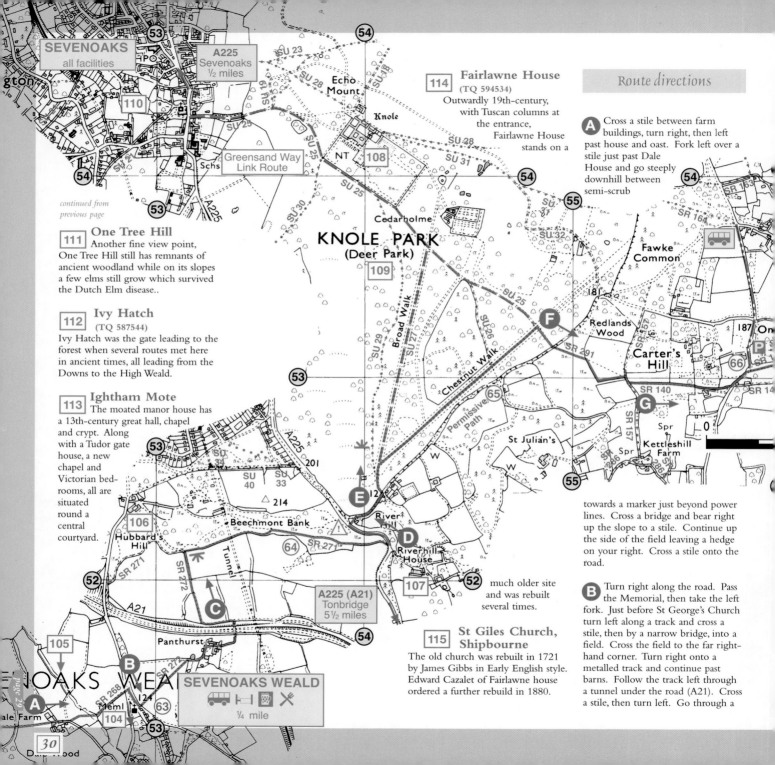

54

SEVENOAKS
all facilities

110

A225
Sevenoaks
½ miles

114 **Fairlawne House**
(TQ 594534)
Outwardly 19th-century,
with Tuscan columns at
the entrance,
Fairlawne House
stands on a

Echo
Mount

Knole

Greensand Way
Link Route

Schs

108 NT

SU 25

Cedarholme

KNOLE PARK
(Deer Park)

109

Broad Walk

Chestnut Walk

65

Permissive Path

St Julian's

W

W

55

Fawke
Common

181

Redlands
Wood

Carter's
Hill

SR 140

G

Spr
Kettleshill
Farm

Spr

66

187

F

continued from
previous page

111 **One Tree Hill**
Another fine view point,
One Tree Hill still has remnants of
ancient woodland while on its slopes
a few elms still grow which survived
the Dutch Elm disease..

112 **Ivy Hatch**
(TQ 587544)
Ivy Hatch was the gate leading to the
forest when several routes met here
in ancient times, all leading from the
Downs to the High Weald.

113 **Ightham Mote**
The moated manor house has
a 13th-century great hall, chapel
and crypt. Along
with a Tudor gate
house, a new
chapel and
Victorian bed-
rooms, all are
situated
round a
central
courtyard.

53

A225

SU
31

SU
40

SU
33

201

214

Beechmont Bank

106

Hubbard's
Hill

SR 271

52

A21

SR 272

Tunnel

C

Panthurst

105

B

SEVENOAKS WEAL

SEVENOAKS WEALD
🚌 🛏 📷 🍴
¼ mile

A

ale Farm

Heml
104

63

53

30

64

SR 271

E 12

River
Hill

D

Riverhill
House

107

52

A225 (A21)
Tonbridge
5½ miles

54

115 **St Giles Church,
Shipbourne**
The old church was rebuilt in 1721
by James Gibbs in Early English style.
Edward Cazalet of Fairlawne house
ordered a further rebuild in 1880.

A Cross a stile between farm
buildings, turn right, then left
past house and oast. Fork left over a
stile just past Dale
House and go steeply
downhill between
semi-scrub

54

SR 163

SR 164

55

towards a marker just beyond power
lines. Cross a bridge and bear right
up the slope to a stile. Continue up
the side of the field leaving a hedge
on your right. Cross a stile onto the
road.

B Turn right along the road. Pass
the Memorial, then take the left
fork. Just before St George's Church
turn left along a track and cross a
stile, then by a narrow bridge, into a
field. Cross the field to the far right-
hand corner. Turn right onto a
metalled track and continue past
barns. Follow the track left through
a tunnel under the road (A21). Cross
a stile, then turn left. Go through a

much older site
and was rebuilt
several times.

gate and walk ahead for 220 yards, leaving the fence on your left.

C Turn right and walk up the field along the old hedge line. At the top cross a stile beside a metal gate, then turn right. Go ahead along a track below Beechmont Bank. Continue for 900 yards until you reach the road (A225). Cross the stile beside the metal gate and turn left.

D Walk up the road for 55 yards to the bend on road where you find the clearest view of traffic each way. Cross the road, turn left and continue uphill for 110 yards. Climb the steps in the bank on your right. Turn right onto the road at the top. Follow the road for 275 yards. Turn left into Knole Park

E Follow the metalled drive as it bends to the right. Ignoring the Broad Walk ahead, turn right into Chestnut Walk and continue for 760 yards. Turn right and go ahead to a road, past a new plantation, fenced, on your left. Leave Knole Park by a swing gate.

F Cross the road. Bear left along a woodland path, then cross a stile into a pony paddock. Turn right and walk to the right-hand corner of the field. Turn left and walk along the scarp edge to a stile. Cross this, then bear right. After 30 yards turn left over a stile.

G Continue ahead along a narrow path between barbed wire fences. When you reach the gravelled driveway of Shepherds Mead bear left to

reach the road. Walk up the road for 165 yards. Turn right up a footpath, then bear right and continue to a clearing and the seat on One Tree Hill.

H Cross to the far left-hand corner of the hill top and follow a broad track for 220 yards to a stile. Cross the stile then bear left and follow the path going steeply downhill above a sharp drop on your right. After 380 yards go down steps to the road. Turn right down a metalled track, then turn left to a stile.

I Cross the stile and follow the track ahead beside the fence.

Cross a stile into the Ightham Mote estate. Continue, first through woodland, then along a field edge. At the end of the field follow the path round the fencing to a stile. Bear right over the stile, down steps. Continue past a house on your left and follow the bridleway for 1½

miles to Mote Farm. Bear left down to the road.

J Turn right. Pass the gates of Ightham Mote then continue for 300 yards to a gate and stile on your left. Cross the stile and walk ahead following the headland path, leaving the hedge on your right. Cross a stile and walk up the left-hand side of a field. At the top turn left over a stile. Follow the woodland path, ignoring all side turns, to reach a stile after 440 yards.

K Cross the stile and walk ahead down a field going to the right of an oak tree. Turn left at the bottom. Walk beside a new plantation to a farm track, then turn right. Cross a stile to the left of a track then bear right across a field recently planted with trees to a stile in the far hedge and cross. Bear left to a stile opposite and cross. Turn left and walk to a gate in the wall of St Giles' Church. Walk to the left of the church and go ahead through a lych gate to the road (A227).

L Cross the road, leaving The Chaser Inn to your right and walk

ahead beside Shipbourne Common. At the far end follow the bend in the road for 30 yards, then turn left beside no 1, New Cottages. Walk along a broad grassy track to go through a wooden kissing gate ahead.

I Kilometre *I Mile*

© Crown Copyright. LA076708/97/05

Section Five

ACROSS THE MEDWAY GAP
shipbourne Common
~ Sutton Valence

DUNK'S GREEN

corner cross a stile and negotiate a slab of stone. Walk ahead to the road, leaving the hedge to your right.

C Turn left along the road. At the junction of Long Mill Lane and Roughway Lane walk ahead down the road past The Kentish Rifleman, leaving it on your right. Cross the bridge over the River Bourne and continue along the road for 220 yards. Just after cottages on

Route directions

A Walk along a broad grassy track to go through a wooden kissing gate ahead. Follow the path down the field. Cross a stream at the bottom on a broad field bridge and walk ahead uphill. Continue past the front of Fairlawne Home Farm to a road.

B Cross the road, go over a stile and continue ahead across a field towards woods. Cross a stile into the woods, then follow the path downhill to a stile. Cross this, then bear right to the far right-hand corner of the field. At the field

your right turn right over the stile into a field.

D Follow the path to the left-hand corner of a field ahead. Keeping the same line continue between young fruit trees. Turn right after 220 yards between the orchard and a line of trees. Walk beside the tree-line, leaving it on your left, for 160 yards. Turn left over a grass field bridge into the next field and follow the field path downhill to a stream at the bottom.

E Cross a field bridge over the stream and bear left up the slope

Map 5a

shipbourne Common (TQ 597523) ~ Moat Wood (TQ 670513)
5¼ miles, allow 2½ hours

between young trees. When you reach a fence, follow the path to continue up the left side of a field beside the fence. After 25 yards turn left over a stile. Bear right down the next field. Cross a stream, then walk uphill to an old gateway to the left of trees. Continue along the path to a stile and cross it to the road.

the path up the slope to the right. Cross a stile and walk ahead, with a windbreak on your left, to a stile at the far end.

H Cross the stile, then turn half left to continue along a broad track for 275 yards.

right-hand corner. Cross two stiles then walk up a broad track to the road (A26).

J Cross the road. Turn right, then, after 60 yards, turn left up an old road. Go over a stile and cross the road. Walk up the lane ahead for 440 yards. Where the lane bears right go up steps in the wall opposite. Go over a stile into the churchyard.

stile, then follow a grassy path between trees and fence to an open field. Continue to the stile ahead and cross, opposite the gate to Roydon Hall. Turn right and walk along the road for 250 yards.

L Turn left up a stony, becoming grassy, path between trees to a field. Continue ahead along field edge, keeping the fence to your left. Bear left and continue along a broad track as it goes between fences. Go ahead to a stile leading into Moat Wood. Follow the clearly defined path as it winds through the woodland.

F Turn left along the road. After 30 yards turn right up some steps, then walk along a footpath, first going between a fence and a hedge, then leaving new orchards on your left. Cross the end of the farm track at the junction with the Wealdway and follow the path ahead, leaving the tree-line to your right and with orchards on your left. Bear right at the end of the field and go down to a broad farm track. Turn left.

G Continue along the farm track to the road beside East Lodge. Turn left. Follow the road as it bends right. Just after the bend take

When the track swings right go ahead through a metal kissing gate onto the Green at West Peckham. Cross the Green and walk ahead along the road to the right of the church. At the junction with Forge Lane, continue along Mereworth Road for 275 yards.

I Turn right at Duke's Place Farmhouse and walk along a farm road. Where this road turns right go ahead along a grass path to a field. Follow the path across the field. Turn right along the field edge. After 195 yards turn left over a stile into woodland, then turn right. Cross a bridge over a stream. Walk up to a stile, cross this, then walk up the field ahead to the far

Turn right, then left to go round the church. Continue to the far right-hand side of the churchyard 45 yards beyond the lych gate.

K Go through a gap in the churchyard wall and walk downhill outside the wall. Cross a stile into a field. Turn through 45 degrees and follow the path to the far left-hand hedge. Turn right along the field edge, then left over a stile. Turn right, walk along a narrow path to a stile. Cross the

Interesting features

116 Old Soar Manor
A manor house built between 1271 and 1299, this ragstone building has an important two-storey solar and a chapel.

117 The Bourne
People settled on the slopes beside the Bourne from Palaeolithic times. Finds include artefacts from the Stone Age, a Bronze Age axe and some Iron Age pottery.

118 Roughway
From the early 19th century the mills beside the Bourne produced high quality paper, specially selected for postage stamps, bank notes and postal orders.

119 Roman villa
A statue of Minerva was found at one of two Roman villas excavated near Roughway.

120 Hamptons
The white cupola seen from the Greensand Way surmounts the stable block at Hamptons, a Palladian-style house built in 1813 by R.W. Jearrad, designer of many buildings at Cheltenham.

121 Oxen Hoath
First built in the 17th and 18th centuries, Sir William Geary had Oxen Hoath redesigned in 1813 to house a collection of French furniture.

122 Wealdway
Devised by the Ramblers Association, this long-distance walk runs for 80 miles between Gravesend and Eastbourne.

123 Lime Avenue
Fine lime trees used to line the avenue leading from West Peckham to Oxen Hoath. They all fell in the 1987 storm.

124 West Peckham
John de Peckham was granted the manor by the Clare family of Tonbridge but the name best known connected with the village was that of the Colepepers who were the first to build a house at Oxen Hoath

125 St Dunstan's Church
The church dates from Saxon times, when part of the tower was built. Inside are memorials to the Colepepers and the Gearys.

126 Duke's Place
Land in the parish of West Peckham was granted to the Knights of the Order of St John of Jerusalem in 1337. Duke's Place, not built until around 1460, became an important centre for the Order.

127 Yotes Court
The name of this 17th-century house, recorded on the 1769 map as Yokes Court, is linked to the amount of land which could be ploughed by a pair of oxen.

128 Fish ponds
An old dam, built of brick, created the fish ponds used by Yotes court.

129 St Michael's Church, East Peckham
East Peckham moved from this original site on the hill to its present site beside the Medway. The church is now maintained by the Redundant Churches Fund.

130 Roydon Hall
This house was first built in 1535 and developed by Sir Roger Twysden and his son in the 17th century. The crow-stepped gables and the chimneys survive from the early building.

Old Soar Manor

Map 5b

Moat Wood (TQ 6705 13) ~ South of Coxheath (TQ 743505)
5 ¾ miles, allow 3 hours

Interesting features

131 Hampstead Lock
This is the deepest of ten locks along the Medway Navigation. The canal links two points on the River Medway to avoid a loop in the river.

132 Anchor Inn
The inn has stood here since around 1780 when the canal was first constructed, providing for barges while they waited for their turn to negotiate the lock gates.

133 Twyford Bridge
The medieval 'bridge of the two fords' spanning the River Medway has brick refuges and pointed cutwaters.

134 The Lees
Remembered by the poet Edmund Blunden as a scene of cricket matches, The Lees, once marshland, served as common land owned by the Lord of the Manor.

135 Town Bridge
Measuring 33 yards, to span both marsh and the River Beult, this ragstone bridge has seven arches and is considered the longest medieval bridge in Kent.

136 Church of St Peter and St Paul, Yalding
The lead cap and vane, dated 1734, and red brick round the windows disguise the fact that much of this church really dates from the 13th century.

137 Lock-up
The studs on the door of this tiny building help to identify the place as the village lock-up.

138 Buston Manor
A medieval building is enclosed in this substantial manor house. The red and blue chequer bricks, added in the late 17th century reflect the wide variety available from the Wealden clays.

139 Weavers
Set in the complex of buildings which once formed Barn Hill Farm, half-timbered Weavers is said to have belonged to a Flemish weaver in the 17th century.

140 Barn Hill
This property has been prominent on the hillside since the early 17th century.

141 Reservoirs
The spring line between the Greensand and the underlying clays has afforded good opportunities for storing water for irrigation.

142 Orchards
Orchard patterns have changed many times over the years but the well-drained soils here, with gentle slopes and the Atherfield Clay only a few feet below, have over many years produced good fruit.

Twyford Bridge, Yalding

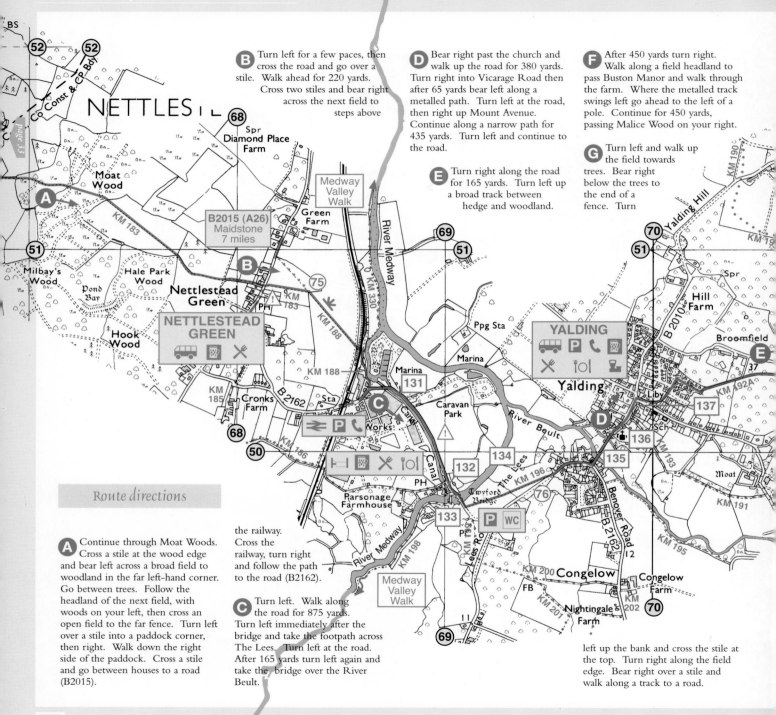

NETTLESTE...

Spr
Diamond Place
Farm

Moat
Wood

Milbay's
Wood

Hale Park
Wood

Pond
Bay

Hook
Wood

Nettlestead
Green

Green
Farm

Medway
Valley
Walk

B2015 (A26)
Maidstone
7 miles

NETTLESTEAD
GREEN

River Medway

Ppg Sta

Marina

Marina

Caravan
Park

River Beult

YALDING

Yalding

Yalding Hill

Hill
Farm

Broomfield

Liby

Sch

Moat

Cronks
Farm

Sta

Works

Canal

The Lees

Congelow

Congelow
Farm

Parsonage
Farmhouse

Twyford
Bridge

Medway
Valley
Walk

River Medway

Lees Ro

Nightingale
Farm

B Turn left for a few paces, then cross the road and go over a stile. Walk ahead for 220 yards. Cross two stiles and bear right across the next field to steps above

D Bear right past the church and walk up the road for 380 yards. Turn right into Vicarage Road then after 65 yards bear left along a metalled path. Turn left at the road, then right up Mount Avenue. Continue along a narrow path for 435 yards. Turn left and continue to the road.

E Turn right along the road for 165 yards. Turn left up a broad track between hedge and woodland.

F After 450 yards turn right. Walk along a field headland to pass Buston Manor and walk through the farm. Where the metalled track swings left go ahead to the left of a pole. Continue for 450 yards, passing Malice Wood on your right.

G Turn left and walk up the field towards trees. Bear right below the trees to the end of a fence. Turn

Route directions

A Continue through Moat Woods. Cross a stile at the wood edge and bear left across a broad field to woodland in the far left-hand corner. Go between trees. Follow the headland of the next field, with woods on your left, then cross an open field to the far fence. Turn left over a stile into a paddock corner, then right. Walk down the right side of the paddock. Cross a stile and go between houses to a road (B2015).

the railway. Cross the railway, turn right and follow the path to the road (B2162).

C Turn left. Walk along the road for 875 yards. Turn left immediately after the bridge and take the footpath across The Lees. Turn left at the road. After 165 yards turn left again and take the bridge over the River Beult.

left up the bank and cross the stile at the top. Turn right along the field edge. Bear right over a stile and walk along a track to a road.

H Turn right and go downhill past Barn Hill Farm. After 275 yards turn left along the driveway below Weavers and Barn Hill Oast and

right along a path between hedge and coppice. Continue to cross-tracks. Turn right.

K After 20 yards turn left over a stile and walk ahead along a

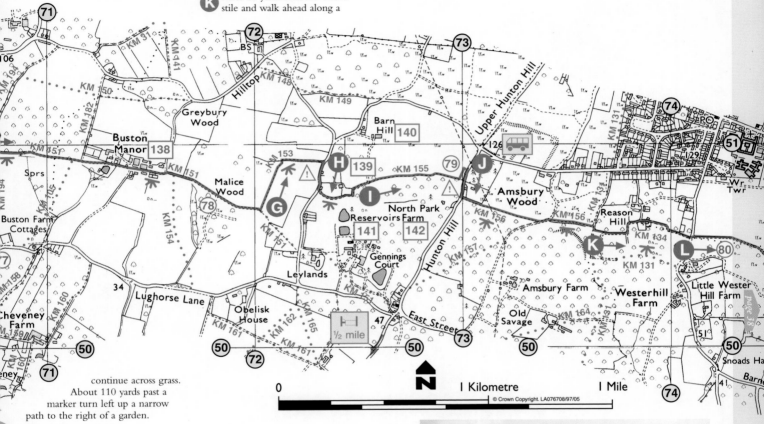

continue across grass. About 110 yards past a marker turn left up a narrow path to the right of a garden.

I Turn right at the top and walk below orchards along an old metalled track. Where the track swings left go ahead on grass. Follow the path ahead between orchards to a stile, then turn left along a path to the road.

J Turn right, then, after 120 yards, turn left up steps set in the bank. Walk along the headland with the fence on your left. Follow the sign half left onto a farm track then bear

fenced headland. Turn left along a farm track at the end of the field. Follow a farm track for 35 yards then turn right. Continue ahead past Reason Hill Oast, then past a clearing beside houses. Turn right downhill for 20 yards. Swing left and walk ahead to a stile leading onto the road.

L Turn left then after 10 yards then right over a stile and walk ahead with a windbreak on your left.

Cottage at Yalding

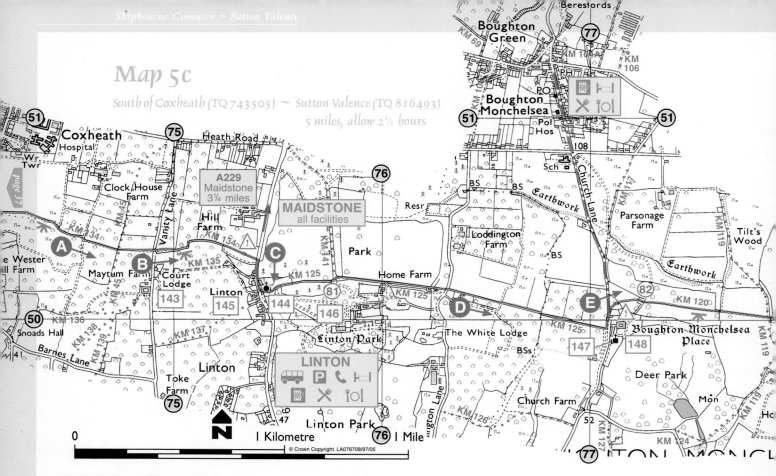

Map 5c

South of Coxheath (TQ 743505) ~ Sutton Valence (TQ 816493)
5 miles, allow 2½ hours

© Crown Copyright. LA076708/97/05

Route directions

A Continue ahead at cross-tracks. Go over a stile in the hedge and continue ahead over rough ground to the far left-hand corner of the field. Cross a bridge over Vanity Lane.

B Go ahead along a path through an orchard and through a line of beech trees. Follow the path ahead through another orchard to the left-hand corner of a thorn hedge. Go through a gap in the hedge and continue along a path with woodland on your right. Enter another orchard and follow the path between trees, bearing right. Cross a stile in the hedge onto the road (A229).

C Turn right and walk downhill. Just before The Bull Inn cross the road onto cobble stones. Enter the churchyard by the gate on the right-hand side. Follow the path round the south side of the church to a metal kissing gate in the far left-hand corner. Walk along the path to cross the driveway leading to Linton House. Continue along the footpath, through a metal kissing gate and ahead to cross the road beside Loddington Oast.

D Follow the footpath ahead, then continue along a headland above orchards. Cross a farm track, then walk to the left of a windbreak. Cross a stile at the end of the orchard. Continue between fences with

orchard on your right. Bear left and follow the path down steps to road above Boughton Monchelsea Church.

E Cross the road and follow a path left and round to your right, below the wall of Boughton Monchelsea Place. Cross the car park into a field. Cross the field. Go over a drive and walk ahead along a broad field path towards trees. Continue through a shaw, and follow the path for 650 yards.

F Pass a parking area on your right. Go through a metal kissing gate beside a double wooden gate. Cross a metalled drive, go through another kissing gate and

cross a stile into a field. Cross the field. Go alongside a metal fence on your right to a stile. Cross this, go through a wooden kissing gate ahead and turn right along Wierton Road. Turn left along East Hall Hill.

G At a bend in the road turn left into an orchard, then immediately right along the hedge line. Turn left through a wind break then continue for 380 yards between trees. Go down steps, turn right then, after 10 yards, take the left fork up a slope. Continue along a broad track between windbreak and barbed wire fence above orchards.

H After 200 yards bear left down a slope to join a rough metalled track. Turn right just before a broad double gate. After 10 yards bear right down a steep path. Follow this down steps, beside a fence above orchards, then over a small bridge and up to an orchard. Turn left up to a steep bank, then right to a road beside Ivy Cottage.

I Continue ahead along the road for 875 yards. Cross the end of Church Road. In 165 yards turn left

continue along the south side of the playing field above the town.

Interesting features

143 **Court Lodge** Seen from the terrace of The Bull, and just one of several Wealden houses along the ridge, Court Lodge has timbers which were felled between 1496 and 1531.

144 **St Nicholas' Church** Built in 1860, using local ragstone, the church contains an outstanding collection of monuments, especially to the Mayne and Mann families, all preserved from the former building.

145 **Linton** Tall chimney stacks are the hall-mark of Linton's estate cottages built in Tudor style in the mid-19th century.

146 **Linton Park** Robert Mann started this huge house in the 1730s. He adapted the building to the scarp slope by building two storeys above and three below. Thomas Cubitt added a third floor in the 1820s.

147 **St Peter's Church, Boughton Monchelsea** The medieval lych gate has a crown-post roof and is thought to be the oldest one in England.

148 **Boughton Monchelsea Place** Robert Rudston bought the manor from Thomas Wyatt in 1551. In 1554 he had to forfeit the house for taking part in his friend's rebellion but bought it back on his release.

149 **Outbuilding** This square building, timber-framed, part brick-clad, part rendered with lathe and cement, was built in the 17th century, or earlier, and may have been a mortuary.

150 **St Michael's Church, Chart Sutton** The west tower was rebuilt in the 14th century, the nave in the 18th century and the chancel in the 19th century, with ragstone taken from local quarries

151 **Sutton Valence** The school in this small hill town was founded in 1578 by William Lambe, a wealthy clothworker. The almshouses in the High Street were also built by him.

152 **Sutton Valence Castle** The Normans built a castle here in the 12th century to keep watch over the Weald where two routes, used since at least Roman times, came up the scarp and converged to the north west of Sutton Valence.

up a metalled footpath. Walk ahead through the churchyard then turn right to a wooden gate in the far right-hand corner.

J Turn right and continue ahead along a farm track between fields. Bear right down a gravel track. Turn left then cross the road (A274) and turn right towards The King's Head at Sutton Valence.

K Just before The King's Head turn left. Walk up an old metalled track between houses. Continue below the school, then

Section Six

THROUGH ORCHARDS TO SANDSTONE HEATH

Sutton Valence ~ Godinton Park

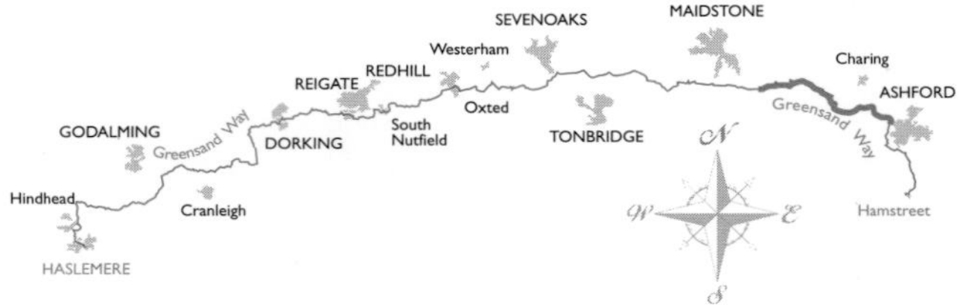

Map 6a

Sutton Valence (TQ 816493) ~ Pope Hall Cottage (TQ 889489)
5 miles, allow 2½ hours

Route directions

A At far corner of the playing field go ahead between trees along a sandy path, then turn left onto a road. Walk ahead to cross roads. Go over the stile in the far left-hand corner and bear left across the field. Cross a track into a field then continue ahead to a stile. Cross the stile and walk along the road ahead to a T-Junction at Charlton Lane.

B Cross the stile ahead. Walk down the left side of the field, to the bottom of the combe, going ahead through the gates, then follow the track uphill to a gate at top. Turn left up the road.

C After 100 yards turn right opposite Morry House and go up a broad track between buildings to enter a hop garden. Walk ahead along a broad track. Go through a gap in the hedge into an orchard and continue above a broad field for 550 yards. Where the main farm track swings left, go ahead to a gate. Follow the farm path left, then right, and walk below the walls of the churchyard of All Saints' Church, Ulcombe to reach the road.

D Cross the road. Walk down the path opposite. Cross the stile into woodland. Cross a stream. Leave the woodland, ahead over a stile. Walk ahead, uphill, going over another, and go to a line of trees. Continue ahead, leaving the trees to your right. Cross a stile and make for the far left-hand corner of a field. Turn left over a stile, then right, down steps.

E Turn left up the side of an old orchard. At the top cross a stile onto the road. Turn left. Follow the road for 330 yards. Turn right over a stile in the hedge. Go ahead for 85 yards to a line of trees. Follow the path between them then walk ahead, with the trees to your left. Walk through a gap in the hedge to a small road.

F Cross the road. Bear left across a field to the end of a line of trees in the far left-hand corner. Cross a stile and enter old hazel coppice. Cross another stile. Take a slight turn left, then right, and continue to a stile leading into orchard. Walk along the right hand side of the orchard beside a tall hedge.

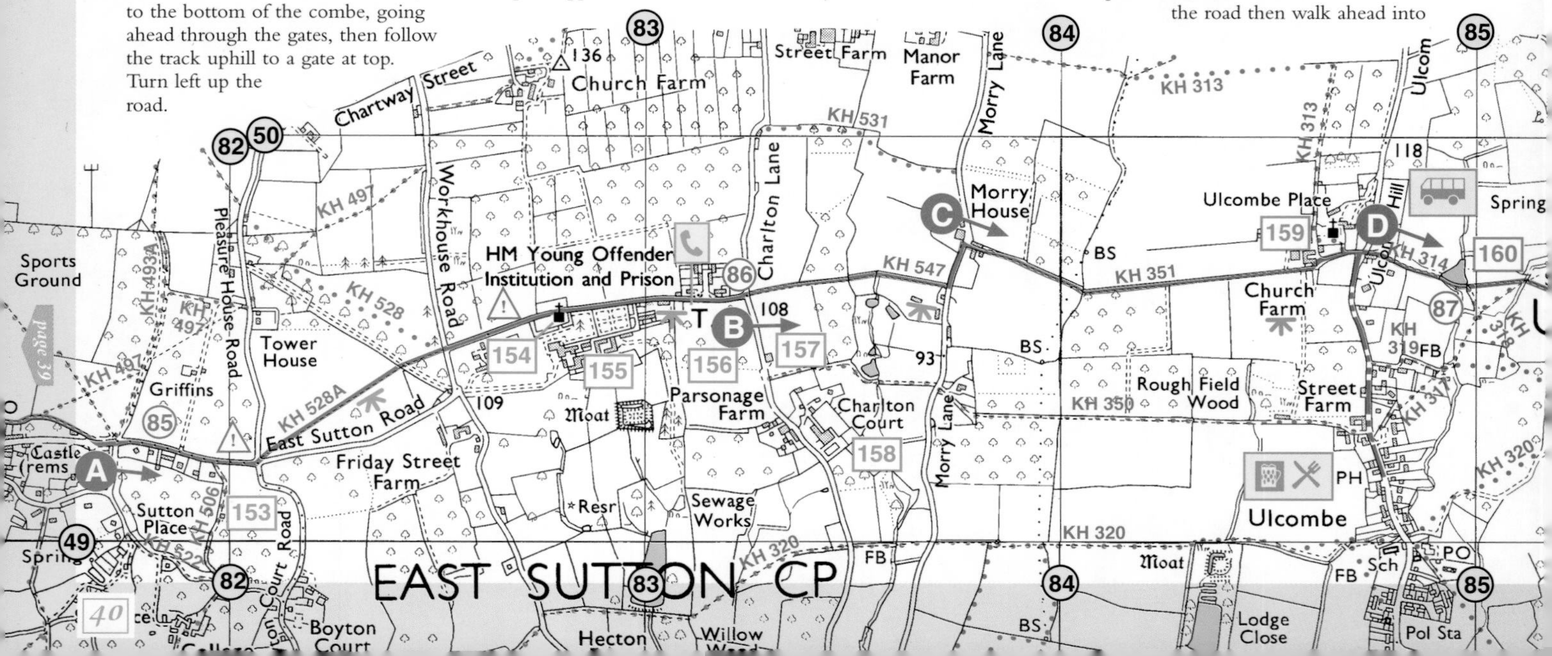

G Cross the stile in the far right hand corner onto a road. Cross the road then walk ahead into an orchard. Bear left and follow the path through orchard to a gap in the trees. Follow the footpath down a slope beside woodland. Continue ahead across open ground to the road at Liverton Street.

H Cross the road to steps set diagonally opposite to your right. Go through a kissing gate and continue ahead along field headlands. After 875 yards , beside Boughton Place, turn right, then left through farm buildings to the road at Boughton Malherbe.

I Turn left. Walk past St Nicholas' Church. Turn right at the bend in the road and follow the metalled track downhill. Continue along a driveway. When the drive bends left, walk ahead between metal fences along a grass track to a gate. Walk past a marker post to the far left-hand corner of the field.

J Cross the stile, then go over a bridge. Bear right, ignoring the path ahead. Join a farm track and follow this path over a ridge. Cross a stile and a bridge then go diagonally across the field to the far right-hand corner by Pope Hall Cottage. Cross the stile and turn left.

K Walk past Pope Hall Cottage garden.

Interesting features

153 Roman road
Traces of a Roman road running through Sutton Valence from Maidstone to Lympne have been found making its way down the terraces of the scarp face.

154 Church of St Peter and St Paul, East Sutton
This once belonged to the priory of Leeds, then served as a chapel to 'Town Sutton' as Sutton Valence was once known. It contains an entire series of memorials to the Filmers.

155 East Sutton Park
Sir Edward Filmer bought the house, now a prison, in 1610 and added to a building already started in Queen Elizabeth's time. The place was besieged in dramatic style by the Parliamentarians in the Civil Wars.

156 Old orchards
In 1735 Thomas Beale agreed to pick all the apples in Sir Edward Filmer's orchards, four acres three roods in all for the sum of £17. He could keep all but three maunds.

157 Oast house
Built in chequered red brick and weatherboarded above, this oast house is one of the best of its kind. It is a reminder of times when the slopes were covered far more widely with hops.

158 Charlton Court
Sir Edward Filmer lived here before purchasing East Sutton Park. The date 1612 on a gable suggests the last year he had work done to it.

159 All Saints' Church, Ulcombe
Unusually large, the church served a college of priests founded in the early 13th century. Today medieval wall paintings may still be seen.

continued overleaf

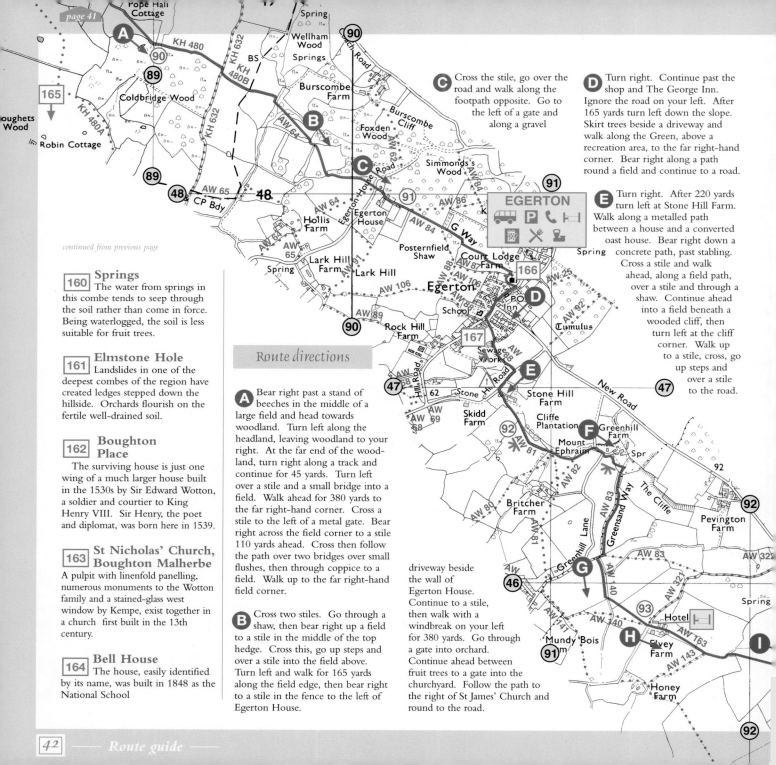

Pope Hall Cottage

Spring

Wellham Wood Springs

Burscombe Farm

Burscombe Cliff

Foxden Wood

Simmonds's Wood

C Cross the stile, go over the road and walk along the footpath opposite. Go to the left of a gate and along a gravel

D Turn right. Continue past the shop and The George Inn. Ignore the road on your left. After 165 yards turn left down the slope. Skirt trees beside a driveway and walk along the Green, above a recreation area, to the far right-hand corner. Bear right along a path round a field and continue to a road.

KH 480

KH 632

BS

KH 480B

KH 632

Coldbridge Wood

165

KH 480A

Oughets Wood

Robin Cottage

Egerton House Road

Hollis Farm

Egerton House

Posternfield Shaw

Court Lodge Farm

EGERTON
166

E Turn right. After 220 yards turn left at Stone Hill Farm. Walk along a metalled path between a house and a converted oast house. Bear right down a concrete path, past stabling. Cross a stile and walk ahead, along a field path, over a stile and through a shaw. Continue ahead into a field beneath a wooded cliff, then turn left at the cliff corner. Walk up to a stile, cross, go up steps and over a stile to the road.

CP Bdy

AW 65

AW 64

AW 65

Lark Hill Farm

Lark Hill

Spring

AW 91

AW 106

AW 84

AW 86

G Way

AW 106

Egerton

P.O Inn

School

167

Tumulus

Spring

AW 92

Rock Hill Farm

Sewage Works

Stone Hill Road

Hill Road

Stone

Skidd Farm

Stone Hill Farm

Cliffe Plantation

Mount Ephraim

New Road

Greenhill Farm

Spr

AW 81

AW 82

AW 83

Greensand Way

The Cliffe

92

Britcher Farm

AW 80

AW 81

Greenhill Lane

AW 83

AW 32

Pevington Farm

92

AW 141

AW 140

AW 321

93

Hotel

Spring

Mundy Bois

AW 140

Elvey Farm

AW 163

91

AW 143

Honey Farm

92

Route directions

A Bear right past a stand of beeches in the middle of a large field and head towards woodland. Turn left along the headland, leaving woodland to your right. At the far end of the woodland, turn right along a track and continue for 45 yards. Turn left over a stile and a small bridge into a field. Walk ahead for 380 yards to the far right-hand corner. Cross a stile to the left of a metal gate. Bear right across the field corner to a stile 110 yards ahead. Cross then follow the path over two bridges over small flushes, then through coppice to a field. Walk up to the far right-hand field corner.

B Cross two stiles. Go through a shaw, then bear right up a field to a stile in the middle of the top hedge. Cross this, go up steps and over a stile into the field above. Turn left and walk for 165 yards along the field edge, then bear right to a stile in the fence to the left of Egerton House.

driveway beside the wall of Egerton House. Continue to a stile, then walk with a windbreak on your left for 380 yards. Go through a gate into orchard. Continue ahead between fruit trees to a gate into the churchyard. Follow the path to the right of St James' Church and round to the road.

160 **Springs**
The water from springs in this combe tends to seep through the soil rather than come in force. Being waterlogged, the soil is less suitable for fruit trees.

161 **Elmstone Hole**
Landslides in one of the deepest combes of the region have created ledges stepped down the hillside. Orchards flourish on the fertile well-drained soil.

162 **Boughton Place**
The surviving house is just one wing of a much larger house built in the 1530s by Sir Edward Wotton, a soldier and courtier to King Henry VIII. Sir Henry, the poet and diplomat, was born here in 1539.

163 **St Nicholas' Church, Boughton Malherbe**
A pulpit with linenfold panelling, numerous monuments to the Wotton family and a stained-glass west window by Kempe, exist together in a church first built in the 13th century.

164 **Bell House**
The house, easily identified by its name, was built in 1848 as the National School

continued from previous page

Map 6b

Pope Hall Cottage (TQ 889489) ~ Coldham Wood (TQ 960459)
6 miles, allow 3 hours

F Turn right. At the bend in the road go over a stile ahead. Follow the path over two stiles to a marker post. Turn right and walk downhill, crossing stiles, for 550 yards.

G Cross a stile. Immediately turn right. Go through a metal gate onto a farm track and turn left over a stile into a field. After 330 yards, at the end of trees, turn left over a stile, then bear left across two fields to a gate onto the track beside Elvey Farm.

H Bear left past Elvey Farm Country Hotel leaving an old granary to your right. Go ahead through a gate and continue along the right side of a field to a gate in the far right-hand corner. Bear slightly right to a marker post by a dyke. Follow the path over a field bridge. Turn left, beside the dyke, then turn back to the north side. Go through a gate. Turn right and continue with the fence on your right.

I At the end of the fence follow the path uphill, aiming to the right of the large red house. Continue through metal gates to a rough metalled track.

J Walk ahead to the road, then turn left. Continue for 380 yards, past the right turn to The Black Horse Inn. Turn right and walk across a playing field to a gap in the far hedge, 33 yards from the right-hand corner. Go ahead through orchard leaving a windbreak to your right. Continue at cross-tracks and walk past Sheerland Farm. Cross a metalled track. Bear left and continue to a metalled lane.

K Cross the lane and continue ahead beside an old wall, then over stiles across a field and along a track. Go through a gate set in a wall. Walk up a slope into orchard. Walk ahead to a windbreak just beyond a broad track. Cross the stile. Turn left into old orchard. Follow the windbreak inside the orchard for 110 yards.

L Turn right towards the orchard centre, then, after 55 yards, turn left and walk to a stile in the windbreak. Cross, then continue through open orchard walking ahead between young fruit trees to the far

left-hand corner of the old estate wall. Go down steps to the road opposite The Swan Inn.

M Turn right along the road, past St Mary's Church. Turn left over a stile after 220 yards and bear right up a field, crossing stiles, to follow a track to the left of houses. Cross a small bridge and go over a stile. Skirt a garden, then turn right along a farm track, into a drive and leaving a pond to your left. Go past Forstal Farm House.

N Turn left. Go ahead past the village green and continue along Ram Lane. After 220 yards turn left through a gateway into a field. Bear right and walk to the far side. Cross a lane and enter Coldham Wood. After 110 yards bear left downhill.

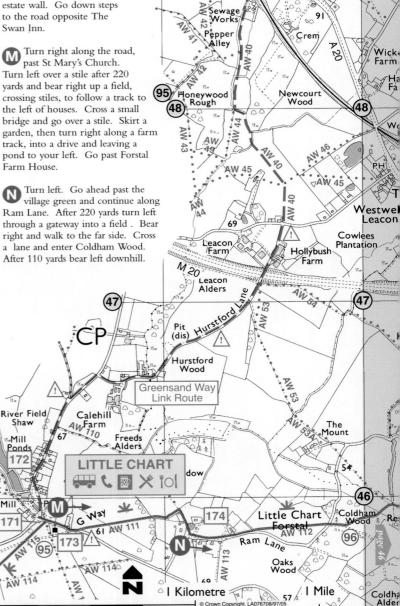

page 45

© Crown Copyright. LA076708/97/05

Interesting features

165 Coldbridge Farm (TQ 885479)
The stone farmhouse standing within an earthwork and outer ditch forms part of a moated castle built in the 14th century, sometime after 1314.

166 St James' Church, Egerton
The church was rebuilt in the 14th century, the tower with its beacon turret added in the 15th century. A crown-post roof to the nave survived 19th-century restoration.

167 Cliffs
The outcrops here and south of Egerton were formed by weathering after landslips.

168 St Nicholas' Church, Pluckley
Inside this 13th-century ragstone church are brasses and monuments to the Malmains and the Dering family. The one of Richard Malmains, dated 1440, is genuine. The others were designed several centuries later.

169 Surrenden Dering
The house built by Sir Edward Dering in the 1630s stood in the centre of the parish. Built on the H-plan it had a series of shaped gables. Dering 'lucky' windows installed in the 19th century failed to save it from fire in 1952.

170 Walnut Tree Farm
Grapes now grow again on the slopes above Walnut Tree Farm. Little Chart was one of the areas in Kent noted for its vines in Tudor times.

171 Park Wall
The brick wall opposite The Swan Inn was built in the 17th century to surround the 350-acre deer park which surrounded Surrenden Dering.

172 Mill ponds
The mill ponds by the old ford across the River Stour powered a water mill where paper was made from 1771. Today Ford Mill still produces paper.

173 St Mary's Church, Little Chart
The church was built in 1955 to replace the medieval church almost entirely destroyed by bombing in the Second World War. The ruined tower of the old church stands ⅔ mile to the north west beside the Pluckley-Charing road.

174 Chart Forstal
H E Bates, author of 'Flying Officer X' and 'The Darling Buds of May', lived at The Granary from 1931 until his death in 1974.

St Mary's Church, Little Chart

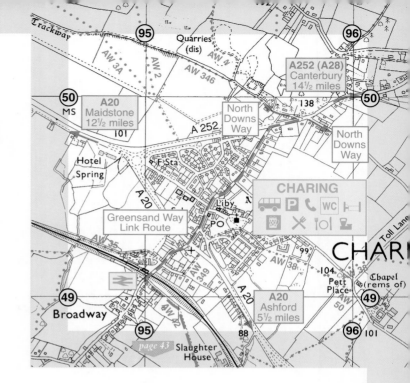

CHARING

North Downs Way

North Downs Way

A252 (A28)
Canterbury
14½ miles

A20
Maidstone
12½ miles

A 252

Greensand Way
Link Route

Hotel
Spring

A20

Liby

PO

Broadway

A20
Ashford
5½ miles

Slaughter
House

Pett
Place

Chapel
(rems of)

Quarries
(dis)

Trackway

Toll Lane

page 43

page 43

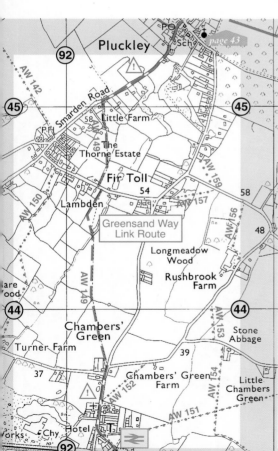

Pluckley

page 43

Sch

PO

Smarden Road

Little Farm

The
Thorne Estate

Fir Toll

Lambden

Greensand Way
Link Route

Longmeadow
Wood

Rushbrook
Farm

Chambers'
Green

Turner Farm

Chambers' Green
Farm

Stone
Abbage

Little
Chambers
Green

Hotel

PH

Chy

orks

0   1 Kilometre   1 Mile

© Crown Copyright. LA076708/97/05

N

Cottage at Little Chart

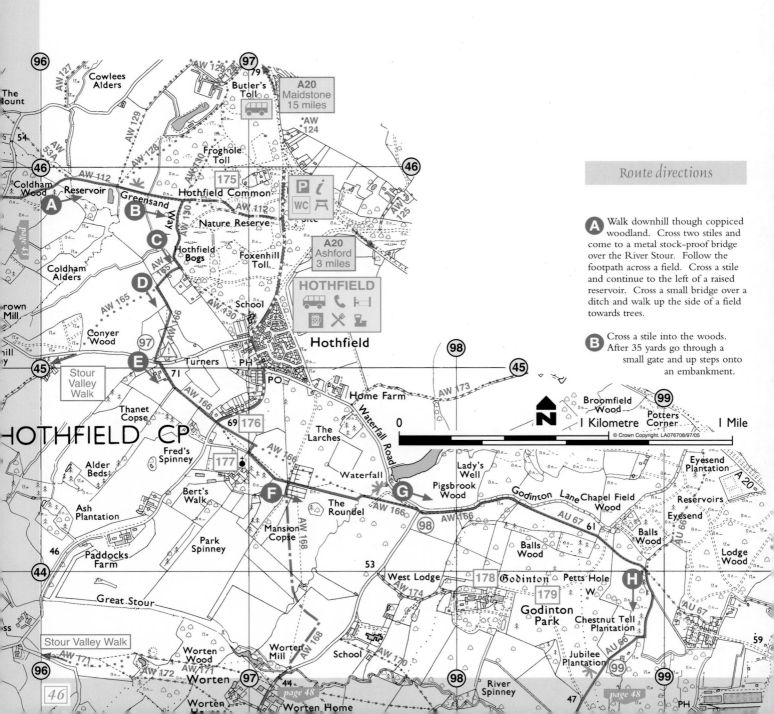

Route directions

A Walk downhill though coppiced woodland. Cross two stiles and come to a metal stock-proof bridge over the River Stour. Follow the footpath across a field. Cross a stile and continue to the left of a raised reservoir. Cross a small bridge over a ditch and walk up the side of a field towards trees.

B Cross a stile into the woods. After 35 yards go through a small gate and up steps onto an embankment.

Map 6c

Coldham Wood (TQ 960459) ~ Godinton Park (TQ 986434)
3 miles, allow 1½ hours

Continue through the wood and onto open heathland. Turn right by a marker post at cross tracks. Continue along a raised concrete path through Hothfield Bogs. Leave Hothfield Common by a small gate.

C Turn left and walk for 110 yards along a broad track. Turn right over a stile and through a gate. Go ahead to a double stile in a tall hedge. Cross into a field.

D Turn left and walk up the headland leaving fence and hedge to your left. At the corner of the field cross a stile. Go ahead to the middle of the next field, then bear right to cross a stile in the far right-hand corner. Cross the stile immediately to your left on the corner, then continue on this line over two more stiles to reach the driveway of Ragstone Barn and the road.

E Turn left along the road, then turn right over a stile and walk up the right-hand side of the field. Cross two stiles to reach the road. Cross the road and go through a gate into old parkland. Ignoring the metalled path which bears right, go ahead to a stile to the left of a gate. Cross the stile, turn right to the gate, then left down the farm track to a gate.

F Go through the gate. Cross a farm track. Walk ahead down

the right side of a field, then bear left to cross a bridge over a stream. Follow the path up the hillside, over a rough metalled track, and continue to the far left-hand corner by a T-junction of roads.

G Cross the road to steps in the far corner. Go up to a field corner and bear left. Walk along the headland with hedge and road on your left. Continue into woodland. Follow a woodland path then cross a stile into a field. Continue to a metal kissing gate in the far fence 30 yards below woodland. Cross the drive which leads to Godinton House above the gate lodge. Go through the kissing gate opposite and continue to another kissing gate.

H Turn right. Follow the headland beside a tall hedge for 240 yards. Turn right through a large gateway and follow the headland on the upper side of the field. Turn right on the farm track between shaws. Go through a metal kissing gate. Walk diagonally across two fields, going through gates. Bear slightly left. Pass a house on your left and walk towards a broad farm track.

Interesting features

175 **Hothfield Common**
A unique feature in east Kent, Hothfield Common lies on a sandstone plateau which itself lies on impermeable clay. Partly heathland, partly peat bog, the Common is classed as a National Nature Reserve and an SSSI.

176 **Park walls**
James Wyatt designed these walls for the Earl of Thanet who lived at Hothfield Place.

177 **St Margaret's Church, Hothfield**
The decorated tower and the shingled spire of the church are the result of re-building in the 17th century after lightning had destroyed the earlier church.

178 **Godinton House**
The Toke family owned the estate from the end of the 15th century. The red-brick house, which has shaped gables outside and superb panelling inside, was built in 1628 for Captain Nicholas Toke.

179 **Godinton Park**
At the end of a long drive, opposite the house, are the remains of the Domesday Oak which had flourished since Norman times. It split in two and collapsed on 3 September 1939.

Commemorative tree plaque, Hothfield church

Ashford church from the town

Section Seven

OLD TOWNS AND ANCIENT WOODLAND
Godinton Park ~ Hamstreet

Map 7a

Godinton Park (TQ 986 434) ~ East of Great Chilmington (TQ 985 400)
2¾ miles, allow 1½ hours

Go through the gate to the road at Chilmington Green.

D Turn left, then left again by a post box and walk up the road for 220 yards. Turn right over a stile, then join a broad farm track on your right and walk ahead along it for 980 yards.

Interesting features

180 **Chart Avenue** This long avenue was the Tokes' driveway between Great Chart and Godinton House which lay in its parish.

181 **St Mary's Church, Ashford** The central tower, 121 feet high, was built by Sir John Fogge in the 15th century as an addition to an earlier church. It still dominates an expanding town.

182 **Church of St Mary the Virgin, Great Chart** The 14th-century ragstone church contains many monuments to the Toke family, including one of Captain Nicholas Toke, in full armour, with his five wives.

183 **Pest House** The purpose of 'the house at the churchgatt' has never been clear. Never a Pest House, in reality it is more likely to have been a rector's residence or possibly a rest house.

184 **Court Lodge** This outstanding hall house, built in 1313, was once a manor house of Christ Church Priory. It consisted of a hall and service area and had good accommodation at the upper end for the family.

185 **Chilmington Quarry** Now infilled, this quarry once supplied limestone for local building and agricultural use.

Route directions

A Cross the farm track and follow the direct line of Chart Avenue downhill for 980 yards. Cross the railway then continue along the track to pass the cricket field. Bear right onto the Ashford Road at Great Chart. Cross a side road and continue uphill along Ashford Road, as far as the church.

B Turn left opposite the church into Hillcrest Road. At the end of the road go through a heavy metal gate. Bear right across the field to a similar gate on the far side. Cross the bridge over the road (A28),

then go through another metal gate and walk ahead across a cultivated field. At the far side bear slightly left then go ahead into the next field to follow the headland on the right-hand side. Continue past the quarry to the road.

C Turn right and walk along the road for 440 yards. Turn left over a stile just beyond woodland. Walk along a field headland to the far left-hand corner. Cross a stile, turn right and follow the path downhill. Cross another stile and continue to a metal gate. Go through the gate and walk along a broad track past orchard on your left, then past buildings, to a second gate.

Map 7b

East of Great Chilmington (TQ 985 400) ~ Golden Wood (TR 012365)
3 ½ miles, allow 1 ¾ hours

Route directions

A Continue ahead on the broad track. Cross a broad field bridge over a dyke. Turn left along a headland, then right at a transverse dyke. Walk towards the marker post under trees, ahead, to the right of the dyke. Turn left over a field bridge over the dyke and walk north-eastwards with another dyke on your right, to a fence. Turn right and cross the dyke by a narrow bridge.

B Cross the road carefully. Cross the bridge ahead over a dyke beside the road. Cross a stile, then walk across the field towards a stile right of centre in the far fence. Cross a metalled track and go over a stile into the field beyond. Bear half-left across the field to a stock-proof wooden bridge. Cross, then continue over a grassy area for 25 yards to a stile which leads to the road.

C Turn right and follow the road to the cross roads at Kingsnorth. Cross the road and continue ahead up Church Hill. Pass Mouse Hall, beside Church Lane, and the Church of St Michael and All Angels. Continue for 130 yards. Turn right just before the road bends right and follow a track, between hedges. Cross a stile, to the left of a gate then follow the path along the side of the

field to the far left-hand corner. Cross the stile. Bear left across the next field towards a large converted barn to the left of the far right-hand corner. Cross the stile in front of the barn, now called Beech Manor, beside a metal gate.

D Turn right, then left into Bond Farm. Go through a metal gate to the right of a pond, then cross the field to the far right hand corner. Go through a gate into Isaac Wood, bear right to the corner of the wood, then cross a stile into a field. Bear left and cross to the far right-hand corner of this field. Cross the stile and follow the path through a field. Cross an old yard to the far corner, then go through the hedge to the road.

E Turn right, then left at the T-junction. After 40 yards turn right through a gate to the right of a lane. Walk along left-hand side of the field, going right then left, to continue ahead through a gate and alongside the hedge on your left. Turn left onto the lane, then right and continue through a wooden gate into Braeside Farm. Go ahead between shacks and farm buildings then continue up the slope for 100 yards towards a house at the top.

F Ignoring the stiles ahead and to your left, follow the main track

to the right and continue to Lone Barn Farm. At the farm go to the far left-hand side of the yard, Cross a stile, continue on the farm track round a pond, then walk up to a stile to the right of the gate ahead. Cross, then bear right to the far right-hand corner of the field. Cross a stile and continue to the far left corner of the next field, beside woodland. Cross a stile and turn left

Interesting features

186 **Mouse Hall**
This tiny weather-boarded cottage may originally have served as a priest's house. It was built in the 14th century.

187 **Church of St Michael and All Angels**
Built in the 14th century, St Michael's Church contains some fine 15th-century stained glass. A full figure survives of St Michael with the dragon.

188 **Golden Wood**
The woods housed a battery of super-heavy railway guns during the Second World War, sited there against a possible invasion by the Germans.

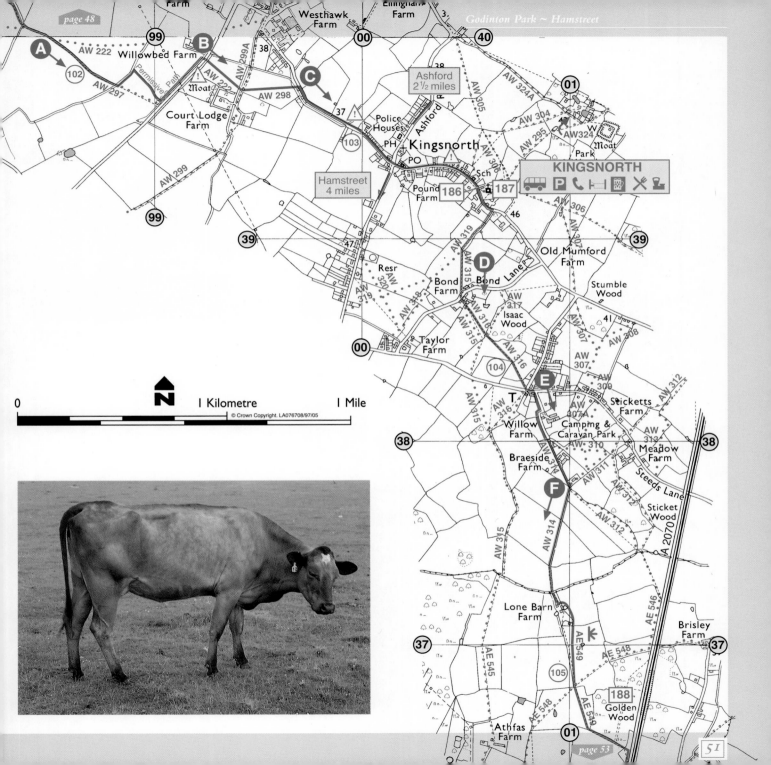

A

AW 222

Willowbed Farm

99

B

AW 299A

38

Westhawk Farm

Eilingham Farm

3.

00

40

01

AW 324A

AW 305

AW 222

Moat

AW 298

AW 297

Permissive Path

Court Lodge Farm

C

37

103

AW 299

99

Ashford 2½ miles

AW 304

AW 295

AW 324

W Moat

Park

Police Houses

PH

Kingsnorth

PO

AW 30

Hamstreet 4 miles

Sch

KINGSNORTH

186

187

39

39

Pound Farm

46

AW 306

47

Resr

AW 320

AW 319

AW 318

Bond Farm

AW 315

D

Bond Lane

Old Mumford Farm

Stumble Wood

AW 317

Isaac Wood

41

00

AW 318

Taylor Farm

AW 316

104

AW 307

AW 308

AW 307

AW 309

AW 312

E

T

Sticketts Farm

AW 315

AW 316

AW 307A

Willow Farm

Camping & Caravan Park

AW 310

Meadow Farm

AW 313

Steeds Lane

38

38

Braeside Farm

AW 14

AW 311

AW 312

Sticket Wood

F

AW 314

AW 312

A 2070

0   1 Kilometre   1 Mile

N

© Crown Copyright. LA076708/97/05

AW 315

AE 546

Lone Barn Farm

AE 549

Brisley Farm

37

AE 545

AE 548

37

105

AE 549

188

Golden Wood

Athfas Farm

01

page 53

51

Royal Military Canal at Hamstreet

Map 7c

Golden Wood (TR 012365) ~ Hamstreet (TR 002334)
2¾ miles, allow 1½ hours

Route directions

A Follow the path beside Golden Wood. Cross a stile and continue to a second stile, then follow the fenced route down to the road (A2070). Turn right and walk beside the road for 150 yards as far as a gate into woodland. Cross the road, then the railway, then walk ahead, along a woodland path to a metalled area beside a house and on to a road.

B Turn right and walk along the road for 350 yards. Where the road takes a sharp left turn go ahead, over a stile, and cross the field to another stile. Cross the stile, go over the road, then over another stile beside a double gate.

C Walk down the side of a field, to the far left-hand corner.

Ignoring the stile to the left, cross the stile ahead. Turn immediately right across a bridge and over a stile. Once over the second stile turn left and walk ahead to the far corner, with tall oaks beside you. In the far left hand corner go ahead over a stile, and continue along a narrow path between woodland and orchard to a stile leading into an open field. Follow the path ahead, through a broad gap into a further field. Continue ahead to a stile. Cross this and turn right along a road.

D At a triangle of grass, turn left down Gill Lane. Continue past the entrance to Gill Farm. Join the Saxon Shore Way and go ahead down a rough gravelled farm track. Where this path goes ahead, bear right, downhill. Go through the gate into Ham Street Woods. Continue ahead downhill ignoring side tracks until you reach a T-junction of tracks. Turn left along a gravelled track to pass the information board.

E Turn right, go over a bridge and walk to the far right hand corner of the car park. Turn right over a stile, then immediately left. Follow the path ahead up the side of the field and over stiles to cross the railway at Hamstreet station. Walk through the station car park. Turn left along the road to reach the cross roads at Hamstreet and the end of the Way.

Interesting features

189 **Ham Street Woods**
National Nature Reserve
These woods form an important remnant of ancient woodland. Maintained as a National Nature Reserve, they provide important habitats for wildlife.

190 **Hamstreet**
For centuries this village remained little more than a hamlet in the parish of Orlestone with only three houses. Its growth began with the arrival of the railway in 1851.

191 **Duke's Head Public House**
This pub is named after the Duke of Wellington who stayed here while observing work on the Royal Military Canal.

192 **Royal Military Canal** (TR 004324)
The Royal Military Canal was built between 1804 and 1809 as part of the defences against a possible invasion by the French under Napoleon.

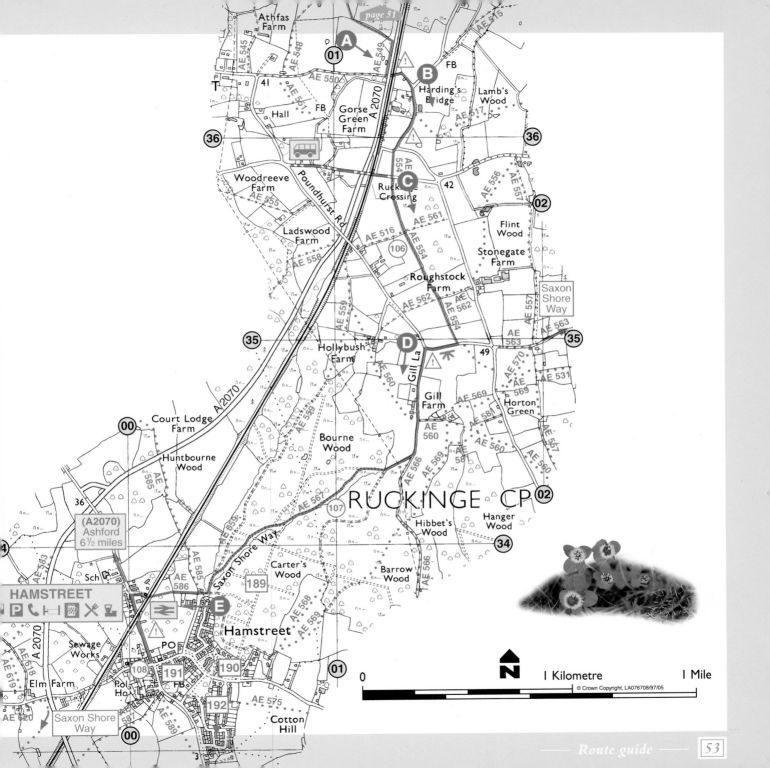

Athfas Farm

AE 545

AE 548

A

01

AE 549

B

FB

Harding's Bridge

Lamb's Wood

41

AE 561

Hall

FB

Gorse Green Farm

AE 550

AE 517

36

36

Woodreeve Farm

AE 555

Poundhurst Rd

AE 554

C

Ruckinge Crossing

42

AE 556

AE 557

02

Flint Wood

AE 561

Ladswood Farm

AE 558

AE 516

AE 554

106

Stonegate Farm

Saxon Shore Way

AE 557

AE 562

Roughstock Farm

AE 562

35

AE 559

AE 562

AE 554

AE 563

35

Hollybush Farm

D

Gill La

49

AE 563

AE 570

AE 569

AE 531

AE 560

Gill Farm

AE 569

Horton Green

AE 560

AE 560

00

Court Lodge Farm

A 2070

AE 560

AE 585

Bourne Wood

AE 539

AE 560

AE 557

Huntbourne Wood

AE 566

AE 569

36

02

AE 561

RUCKINGE CP

107

(A2070) Ashford 6½ miles

AE 583

AE 585

Saxon Shore Way

Hibbet's Wood

Hanger Wood

34

Sch

AE 586

189

Carter's Wood

Barrow Wood

AE 566

HAMSTREET

AE 568

E

AE 569

AE 566

Hamstreet

A 2070

Sewage Works

PO

108

191

190

FB

AE 575

01

Elm Farm

AE 618

AE 619

Pol. Ho.

192

AE 587

AE 589

Cotton Hill

AE 620

Saxon Shore Way

00

3

0   1 Kilometre   1 Mile

N

A Walkers Code

- Always wear suitable clothing and footwear for the season, the weather and the terrain.

- Allow plenty of time to complete your walk; normally reckon on walking 2 or 2½ miles (3·2 or 4 km) an hour.

- Most public paths cross private estates and farmland; enjoy the countryside, but please have regard for its life and work.

- Avoid interfering with or disturbing things which are connected with a farmer's livelihood.

- Always keep to the paths to avoid trespass and remember that you only have a right of passage on a right of way. Walk in single file through a crop.

- Keep dogs under close control at all times and preferably on a lead across farmland.

- Take care when crossing or walking along country roads; keep to the right, in single file and keep a good lookout for traffic.

14. Are you a member of any of the following organis-ations? (Please tick boxes)

Ramblers' Association ☐

National Trust ☐

RSPB ☐

Kent Wildlife Trust ☐

Other walking or countryside organis-ations (write in) ☐

....

....

....

15. Are you a regular or irregular reader of any of the following publications for walkers?

The Great Outdoors ☐

Trail ☐

Country Walking ☐

Other (write in) ☐

....

....

16. How do you gain information about walks and events in the countryside?

Local paper ☐

Tourist information centre ☐

Word-of-mouth ☐

Local radio ☐

District/county council ☐

Library ☐

Country park/visitor centre ☐

Bookshop ☐

Posters/leaflets (where from) ☐

....

Other (write in)

....

....

....

17. Are there any other comments you would like to make either about the route or the guidebook?

....
....
....
....
....
....
....
....
....
....
....
....
....
....
....

18. Having used the Greensand Way guidebook, would you consider purchasing Ordnance Survey maps for other walks?

Yes ☐

No ☐

19. Have you, or do you intend to purchase the Landranger and/or Explorer maps associated with this guidebook?

Yes ☐

No ☐

20. Do you own any Explorer maps?

Yes ☐

No ☐

21. I would like to receive more information about waymarked walks in Surrey and Kent. ☐

I am already listed on the SCC and KCC Countryside mailing list. ☐

Thank you for your help, in return for which we will send you a voucher offering you a 10% discount against selected items from our wide range of countryside and coast products.

Name: *Mr/Mrs/Ms* ....

Address: ....

....

....   Postcode: ....

Tick the box if you would like to receive more information about Ordnance Survey products ☐

Fold 3

BUSINESS REPLY SERVICE
Licence No MA 629

Access and Recreation Officer
Planning Department
Kent County Council
Springfield
MAIDSTONE
Kent
ME14 2LX

Fold 4 Tuck in to flap opposite and post

An industrial past

Chalk from the Downs had been readily available and much in demand from early times, provided the transport was available, to fertilise the heavy clay in the valley. Signs both here and from the later stretches of the Greensand Way of the old quarry sites on the Downs slopes are hard to miss. At Brockham and Betchworth many traces still survive of the quarrying and limeworks which grew up in the second part of the 19th century. Increasing demand for lime for agricultural use in the 1860s led to the foundation of the Dorking Greystone Lime Company, which flourished until the 1960s. The arrival of the railway in 1847 helped the local industry considerably and in 1867 William Finlay, the first owner of the company, who leased the land from the Brodie family, had standard gauge tracks laid to connect with the railway at Betchworth station. The first horse-drawn locomotives were replaced by steam in 1871.

Far less obvious are the sites lower down the slopes, almost in the clay valley itself, where stone was extracted by mining.

For, running under the Downs near the junction of the chalk and clay, lay the seams of Upper Greensand, the malmstone which not only provided much of the building-stone of medieval London and many other places round about, but also stone used to line kilns and ovens and even for scrubbing blocks used by Victorians to scour their steps.

While these bands run almost the entire length of the Greensand ridge they only surface in a way that is practical for extraction for a short stretch. Further west they lie too low, further east the strata are too thin. Between Brockham and Betchworth in the west and Godstone in the east the seams were rich, with tunnels, now no longer used, running for many miles interweaving below the ground.

At Brockham and Betchworth the seams nearest to the surface and most easily mined produce a relatively soft and crumbling stone, called hearthstone. At first it was used for building, and provided some of the stone for repairs to Betchworth church. But its soft and crumbling nature soon made this impracticable and it was sold for

Reigate windmill

scouring blocks. The workings ran under the Downs, where open bays were created as men hacked at the stone, leaving pillars of stone for support. It was heavy work, for the seams ran down at a sharp angle and there was a risk of flooding.

Two other works flourished in the area in the last century: brickmaking in an area of Gault clay between the limeworks at Brockham and the railway station, and sand digging from a pit just north of the village. The area was largely industrial. Today the villages are classed as conservation areas.

After a comfortable walk through an area farmed for many centuries, you reach Reigate Heath, where the Folkestone Sands emerge to create a rare stretch of lowland heath. At first sight this may

seem surprising, with a well-used golf course covering much of the area, that this is an important SSSI, but on the open heath and acidic grassland around the golf course you may find rare birds-foot fenugreek as well as the normal plants found in sandy soils such as ling, bell heather and wavy hair grass. Further away you can see how a natural succession establishes itself. First come scrub and bracken to take over from the open heathland. In turn oak and birch take over, with some pine, and in wet areas, alder.

Reigate windmill

An attractive landmark stands above Reigate Heath, a post mill, built here around 1765 and one of five windmills in the Reigate area alone. The mill ceased working in about 1870 and was converted to a chapel of ease to St Mary's Parish Church, Reigate, in 1880. The post mill was the earliest kind of mill, so-called because the massive post at the centre turns to face the wind. The tower mill of the kind you passed at Ewhurst had developed from the post mill. There only the cap turned with the wind. Not only the clay valley but the top of the Greensand scarp was known for its windmills. Among the many which dominated the skyline you may visualise, especially, a post mill on the ridge just west of Bletchingley, another on the summit of Tilburstow Hill and one at Limpsfield Chart.

The marshy meadows to the north and east of Skimmington

Reigate and North Downs from Reigate Park

are also important for wildlife. These are the only remaining meadows of this kind in Surrey to have escaped modern farming methods. Yorkshire fog grass creates a lush, grey sheen in early summer. Rare orchids may be found. Heron and kingfisher feed by the stream.

Reigate

From the top of Reigate Park you look down on the town of Reigate, once fortified in its castle by the de Clare family of Tonbridge. The town gives its name to the Reigate Stone, often called firestone, which comes close to the surface in this region. From at least the 11th century until as late as the 1960s this was excavated as part of an important mining industry. For a long time it was

used for building and, naturally enough, you can see it used in buildings in Reigate's High Street. Firestone was much used in London in early centuries, most notably for Westminster Abbey and parts of Tower Bridge. But the stone absorbed water and flaked after frost and, like the even softer hearthstone of Betchworth, its use was gradually discouraged. The stone remained in demand throughout the country for hearthstones, and the lining of kilns and ovens.

Fuller's earth

One other well-known commodity from this region was fuller's earth, embedded in the Lower Greensand. The seam which occurs about 20 to 30 feet below the surface between

Nutfield and Bletchingley was considered the best in the country and for several centuries large quantities were excavated here. The absorbent properties of the powder enabled cloth-workers to extract the grease from newly woven cloth. More recently fuller's earth has been used in the oil industry and for use as cat litter. Resources are now running low but some is still extracted.

The growth of the railways

The railway line which runs through South Nutfield from Redhill to Tonbridge, constructed by the South Eastern Railway Company, was one of the first lines to be built. At the time it had considerable social impact. Bringing new settlements to Oxted and creating smaller villages at South Nutfield and South Godstone, it created a social mobility not known before. There was movement between Kent and the Midlands and, when extended to Dover in 1844, the railway enabled travel to the Continent. The line now carries Channel Tunnel freight.

Another railway, less well-known but built much earlier,

was the Grand Surrey Iron Railway. Really only a horse-drawn tramway, it was the first publicly-owned conveyance in England. It started in 1802 from a wharf at the confluence of the Wandle and the Thames at Wandsworth. In 1810 it was extended over the Downs to Bletchingley to serve the chalk quarries and the fulleris earth pits at Merstham and Nutfield.

Bletchingley

The name of Bletchingley, once Blechingley, suggests it was

occupied from Saxon times ('the leah of the people (ingas) of Blaecci'). Certainly the outcrop on the Greensand ridge made it an ideal place for a settlement. Domesday Book recorded one manor, held by the powerful de Clare family of Tonbridge. By the 13th century it was a flourishing market town, with a market, an annual fair, granted in 1283 and fulling and weaving as industries. The de Clares built a castle soon after the Norman conquest. This was rebuilt to a high standard in the 12th century but demolished in 1264 during the wars between Henry III and Simon de Montfort. After the death of the last de Clare, Earl of Gloucester and Hertford, at the Battle of Bannockburn, the population began to move south towards the Weald in search of iron ore.

A Borough by the early 13th century, Bletchingley's population decreased considerably. In the

early 19th century it still sent two members to parliament and was pilloried as one of Cobbett's 'vile rotten boroughs'. Still based on one main street, today it is picturesque, especially at the eastern end where the street opens into what was once the market square, with St Mary's Church and many timbered or tile-hung buildings in the background. Even the inn sign standing on the pavement is a listed monument.

Some of Surrey's watermills were documented in Domesday Book and their popularity continued until the steam mill replaced them in the late 19th century. King's Mill appeared on a map of 1768, doubtless built to take advantage of the rising production of wheat. Other older mills adapted according to the demands of the time, changing from iron production to gunpowder and then to corn-milling.

Leigh Mill

Leigh Mill, Godstone holds particular interest. Here, on the Gibbs Brook, a corn mill was recorded in Domesday Book. The site was used for gunpowder manufacture by the

Evelyn family of Wotton from the late 16th century to 1635 for Queen Elizabeth I, anxious to maintain the gunpowder supplies, had licensed the Evelyns to collect saltpetre throughout most of England and convert it into gunpowder. To keep a constant water supply to turn the wheel the Evelyns dammed the stream further up, so creating the Bay Pond in Godstone. Leigh Mill later reverted to corn-milling. The present brick and weather-boarded building dates from the 18th century.

Leigh Mill Pond is estimated to be 1,500 years old. The combination of the calcareous streams flowing into it from the North Downs with the sandstone base of the Hythe Beds has over the years created a remarkable habitat for wildlife. Horned pondweed, greater duckweed and white water-lily all grow here and the site supports an outstanding number of 54 species of breeding bird, all attracted by the numerous invertebrates. Kingfishers and coots as well as sedge warbler and water rail are all found here. The pond is an important site for breeding wagtails.

Timber framing with hung tiles and brick infill, Bletchingley

Chapter Four

THE GROWTH OF THE COUNTRY HOUSE

Oxted Place ~ Shipbourne Common

From Tandridge the Greensand Way now leads towards Limpsfield and the High Chart. The land here, with common and woodland, was once classed as manorial wastes. Today Limpsfield Common and the woodland of the High Chart form part of an AONB. As you walk over this high ground you catch more glimpses of Downs to the north. You soon reach the County boundary set in 1894, then come first to Crockham Hill, then to Mariners Hill. You pass Chartwell and tiny Frenchstreet then climb to Toys Hill and, soon, Ide Hill, both with panoramic views to the south. Passing Wickhurst

Manor and Sevenoaks Weald you then reach Knole, first built for archbishops, gabled, chimneyed and with mellow ragstone. You find a ragstone mansion again at Ightham, reflected in the moat.

Tandridge

Settlers chose Tandridge for its position on the line where springs emerged at the junction of clay and sandstone and the village grew to hold an important role in medieval times as centre of its Hundred. The Hundreds Knoll to the west of Tandridge Hill Lane, last used in the 18th century, marks the site where the meetings took place. For a while the area was part of

the Surrey industrial belt, but recently fought off plans to extract the last of its fuller's earth. Today Tandridge is largely an agricultural community, its small village running down the scarp face towards the Weald. Intervening history has been varied. To the north, beyond the A25, was an Augustinian priory founded in 1200 AD and built on the site of a Hospital of St James established for the relief of the poor. Tandridge Priory replaced them both in the 16th century. Only fishponds survive from the earliest building.

Still to the north, but nearer to the Greensand Way and well worth the detour, lies St Peter's Church, a Grade I listed building. This attractive church was first built around 1100 AD. Its massive oak beams were installed around 1300 to support the bell tower. Sir George Gilbert Scott lived in Tandridge so it was natural for him to include

St Peter's among his many restorations. Lady Gilbert Scott is buried in the churchyard.

To the south-east lies Tandridge Hall, 'a faire brick house', as described by John Aubrey in 1673.

That was the Tudor building. Much of a later, Georgian building was destroyed by fire during the Second World War. You still see something of its

style in The Lodge, just south of The Barley Mow. The Doric portico incorporated here appears several times in this village.

Ightham Mote

43

Oxted

A mill was first recorded near Oxted on the banks of the River Eden in Domesday Book. It became a water-mill in the mid-19th century. The external undershot wheel was enclosed in 1893 when a second mill was added. This was a roller mill which produced especially fine flour. Oxted, to the south of the A25, another village which first developed on the spring line, is well worth exploring for the 15th and 16th-century houses in the High Street. The three-storey Crown Inn was first built in the late 15th century.

Limpsfield

The Manor of Limpsfield was recorded in Domesday Book and soon after became a manor of Battle Abbey. It was valued before 1066 at £20, by 1086 at £24. At that time it had a mill, a fishery, a church, a four-acre meadow woodland with 150 pigs, three hawks nests in the woodland and 10 slaves. Two stone quarries, worth two shillings a year at the time, continued to be worked until the 18th century, for the rough chert used for roads.

Land owned by Battle Abbey was let to tenant farmers and houses built by these farmers in the 15th century can still be seen. Other houses date from the 17th century, when agriculture was prospering. The 18th century saw the building of some larger houses.

A red clay just below the surface supported considerable industry over the centuries. Pottery had been made and used in Roman times, with a kiln on the High Chart itself. Waste from the pottery sites was often dumped on the slopes to the south of the Chart, at Scearn Bank. Much later the Limpsfield area was particularly well-known for its medieval coarseware pottery.

Brick Kiln Lane is a reminder of the brickworks which flourished here between the 17th and early 20th century. The corner of the golf course now covers the site where the brickearth was dug from clays in the Sandgate Beds. When the Lord of the Manor tried to extend the clay-digging to the Common in 1830 he caused uproar among the Commoners whose rights had existed since the 14th century. The bricks produced were the red variety you see in the area, sometimes surrounding only the doors because of their expense. Some people clearly prospered as a result of the works. The crenellated house at the foot of Wolf's Row was built in 1903 by George Wickham who rented the brick works.

Limpsfield Chart

Limpsfield Chart has seen dwellings grow up over several centuries. Inevitably the railway brought new residents to the

Autumn woods, Crockham Hill

region in the 19th century and The Chart also attracted a number of members of the Fabian Society. St Andrew's Church was built in 1895, its reredos designed in the Arts and Crafts style. But old ways continued for some time. A post mill, installed in the early 19th century stood until 1925, between Windmill Cottage and Mill House.

Kent Hatch, the 'Kent Gate', lies on the line of the Roman road from London to Lewes. A curve in the road here eases the gradient and breaks the otherwise straight line over the woods of Limpsfield Chart to the Ashdown Forest.

Mariners Hill

At Mariners Hill you cross the first of a number of National Trust properties in the area. The land here was partly given to the Trust by Octavia Hill, a 19th-century pioneer social reformer and co-founder of the National Trust who lived at Crockham Hill. You can see her tombstone beside the path leading up to Holy Trinity Church. Her effigy, showing an old lady in a shawl, lies inside the church.

Desirable building land

The County of Kent is particularly rich in country houses. Some, like Knole, built in Tudor times, always displayed grandeur and importance. Others started in medieval times in more modest style but the vast majority of Kent's larger houses were built or rebuilt around older houses in the 17th and 18th centuries as owners and requirements changed. New wealth had come. For some, already established in Kent, a flourishing wool industry and agriculture had helped them prosper. For others the iron industry provided great revenues. Meanwhile city merchants always brought new wealth to the county, especially in the west.

The Greensand ridge was always a favoured place for those seeking land nearer to London. From early on the old estates had gradually been parcelled into smaller estates such as those of Penshurst or Ightham Mote. Land in the Vale of Holmesdale had long since been taken and the Weald was impassable for many months of the year. The Greensand however was reasonably accessible. Manorial land first given to followers of William the Conqueror had changed hands many times and while some 'old' families remained, estates on the ridge were from time to time available for 'newcomers'. Everyone loved the view and as farming practice developed, the land gave them good returns.

As in Surrey you still see the timber-framed houses, the brick infilling, the hung tiles and the weatherboarding. Ragstone was used in early times but only by the wealthier people. In Kent you find many more of the older houses enlarged and from an earlier date. Above all brick, always a sign of some wealth, was now becoming cheaper and was used for a new style of country house along the Greensand ridge, each individual in design and style but all reflecting an increasingly upward mobile group of landowners and gentry.

Chartwell

Chartwell lies in the valley to the east of Mariners Hill. First built in Tudor times, it had been restored in the 19th century, to show much of its early design. Today it is well-known

Statue of General Wolfe, Westerham

as the home of Sir Winston Churchill who bought it in 1924 and lived there until his death in 1965. The house was bequeathed to the National Trust who display it much as it was in the 1930s. On view to the public are Second World War displays in the library. You can also see Churchill's paintings and his collection of porcelain. Further north in Westerham, Churchill is remembered again by a bronze statue, seated and in pensive mood, while not far from him is a statue of General Sir James Wolfe, an earlier resident of the town, who took Quebec in 1759, but died soon after.

Chartwell

45

Frenchstreet

Long before one John le ffrenche came to live at Frenchstreet in Norman times, Iron Age Celts had occupied the upper slopes as a coin hoard found in 1927 in gravel workings revealed. The gold stators, now known as the Westerham Gold, reside in the British Museum. Today there is a small community at the head of this attractive combe. The oast house converted for modern use at Frenchstreet Farm recalls the days when this was a working farm. Old photographs show the oasts used as a cart shed. Today there is no trace of hop growing but sheep still graze the slopes. As you walk you will see miles of new hedging and young trees, planted to restore the woodland.

Frenchstreet Nursery was formerly the kitchen garden and Italian water garden of Weardale Manor. Churchill used to take fruit from the greenhouse to King George VI. Lord Weardale of the Stanhope family built his house on Toys Hill in 1906. The building was prominent on the hilltop and could be seen by aircraft flying into the country even from the Sussex coast. For this reason it was demolished in 1940 to prevent German bombers using it as a guide to nearby Chartwell, a lucky move as a bomb did subsequently hit the site. Today a clump of pines marks the place where Weardale stood.

Toys Hill

At 808 feet Toys Hill is the highest point in Kent. From here you can see Gibbet Hill near the start of the Way and look due south to the Ashdown Forest. These slopes were part of the parish of Brasted and used as common land where swineherds brought their pigs to feed on the acorns. You will see a mixture of woodland management here. Some trees, pollarded to provide fresh growth above the level reached by greedy snouts, pre-date 1853 when the land was enclosed. Coppiced trees, where the new growth was below snout level, date from later, once the grazing ended and it was possible to maintain the new growth generated by cutting back the trees to near-ground level. For a few years after the 1987 storm views could be seen from any point. Today that view has

Emmett's Garden, Ide Hill

already gone. The many young birch saplings have all sprung up in the intervening years.

Ide Hill

Ide Hill grew up in the middle ages as a clearing on the old drovers' road from Brasted to Hever. For centuries the people from the tiny hamlet used to walk to church in Sundridge three miles to the north. Only gradually was this situation remedied. A small chapel was built in 1807 and the church, whose spire you see from all around, was built in 1865. An American family who lived nearby added the blue and gold ceiling in memory of John F. Kennedy.

Many areas around here are designated as SSSIs. As you descend from the highest point you see the changes from the higher ground. On the dry, acidic soil of the plateau you see sessile oak, pedunculate oak, birch, whitebeam and rowan. On the heavier, limey clay you find pedunculate oak again, but here there is a far richer ground cover where wood sorrel, honeysuckle and wood anemone all flourish.

At Wickhurst Manor you see a fine manor house, outwardly Victorian. A closer look reveals a 15th-century stone doorway, the external reminder that the house is one of the many Wealden hall houses to be seen in Kent. Even this doorway may have added after the original house was built. The Victorian house contains within it the medieval hall and a crown-post roof. The peaceful setting belies a stormy past when the occupants became embroiled in a rebellion of some of the gentry of Kent in the 16th century, led by Thomas Wyatt.

Sevenoaks Weald

Sevenoaks Weald was yet another of the tiny Wealden hamlets which proved attractive as more people moved away from London. The Church of St George was built, like most of the village, in the 19th century, the nave and tower earlier, in 1820, the chancel later, in 1872. Portland stone was used, rather than local stone. On the slopes beyond, separated now by the A21, Riverhill House has fine gardens created in the mid-19th century. Here John Rogers, an early member of the Royal Horticultural Society, established plants and shrubs newly introduced to the country in acid soil ideal for their growth. Cedars of Lebanon, Deodar cedars and a Wellingtonia all flourish here.

Knole

Further on, in a thousand acres of parkland, rises Knole taking its name from the knoll on which it stands. This large mansion was first built of local ragstone in 1456 by Thomas Bourchier, Archbishop of Canterbury. His successors continued what he had begun. Archbishop Cranmer yielded the place to Henry VIII who then enlarged it. In her turn Elizabeth I gave it to her cousin, Thomas Sackville, whose descendants still live here. Much of the roof, the shaped gables and the chimneys you see across the park from the Chestnut Walk were part of a rebuilding programme of 1605. The house contains a unique collection of rare and important 17th-century furniture and textiles. Among many other treasures you will find paintings by Reynolds and cartoons by Raphael.

Knole Park

The familiar and often inquisitive deer in the historic park have grazed the land so extensively that they have prevented a good shrub layer from forming and so limited the growth of young trees. The grassland is the most important stretch of acid grassland in Kent, unimproved by fertilisers. Dead wood, to which much was added after the 1987 storm, supports important fungus and lichen. Here you will find the best collection of invertebrates in Kent.

Ightham Mote

Knole was built by an archbishop and his successors, then owned by sovereigns before the Sackvilles arrived. It represents the grand style. Another mansion along the Way, Ightham Mote, is also unique. Situated in a secluded valley, its four quarters surrounding an inner courtyard and the whole surrounded by a moat, it is one of England's most attractive smaller manor houses dating from the early 14th century. Its first builder is

unknown but Sir Thomas Cawne was its first recorded owner. He lies in style, in full armour, a small lion at his feet, in St Peter's Church in Ightham village. The great hall, crypt and two solars were built in the 14th

Ightham Mote

century. Other owners followed and, over the next three centuries added the west range and gate tower, a new chapel, library, drawing room and Victorian bedrooms. Never a place of siege or storm, the moat, gate tower, and its crenellations, were built for status, not defence.

Chapter Five

ACROSS THE MEDWAY GAP
Shipbourne Common ~ Sutton Valence

The Way now takes you over the lower slopes of the ridge, through arable and pasture around Shipbourne and Fairlawne Home Farm and below the orchards and hop gardens around Plaxtol. From there the path leads on to the lands once owned by the Colepepers and Gearys and past their house at Oxen Hoath. The Church of St Dunstan at West Peckham has many memorials to both these families. Another last climb takes you past the redundant Church of St

Michael at East Peckham, wonderfully situated on a spur overlooking the Weald. Nearby is Roydon Hall, once home of a prominent Royalist in the Civil War. Then comes a steady walk into the Medway valley, across the Medway gap and on to the eastern slopes above Yalding. Now you are once more on the Hythe Beds with the scarp below you. You are greeted by a succession of orchards, and fine houses on old manorial lands. Through Linton, past

Boughton Monchelsea and on to Chart Sutton and Sutton Valence, the houses link with the villages to portray many centuries of history along the eastern scarp.

Twyford Bridge, Yalding

Shipbourne

The Fane family held the manor of Shipbourne from the end of the 16th century. One of the family, Henry Fane, later to change the name to Vane, and to be knighted in 1620, took an increasingly active part in politics. To match his rise in rank he bought the mansion of Fairlawn. He later became embittered with royalty, alienated all his friends and family and retired to his castle in Durham from where he had first come. His son inherited both estate and grievance and, unusually for a landowner in Kent, followed the Parliamentarian cause in the Civil War. Samuel Pepys watched his execution on Tower Hill on 16 June 1662.

The family's fortunes took a turn for the better during the next century, during which time the house at Fairlawn, later Fairlawne, grew considerably. No money was spared in its development, and when a new wing was burnt down it was rebuilt, only to be rebuilt again after a second fire.

St Giles' Church is Early English in style with splendid gargoyles winging their way outwards from the four corners of the tower. It was rebuilt at the Vane's expense in 1771-2, then by Edward Cazalet, a later owner of Fairlawne, in 1880-81. If the church is open it is worth looking at the carving and the bright stencilling on the walls inside. Other features include a carved, stone pulpit and an elaborate monument to the first Lord Barnard and his lady, with their daughter reclining at their feet.

The Cazalet family affected Shipbourne in other ways, leaving Shipbourne with attractive estate houses, an attractive inn, The Chaser, beside the Green and immaculate Fairlawne Home Farm. Major Peter Cazalet was trainer of racehorses to HM the Queen Mother.

At Roughway you are reminded by the inn, The Kentish Rifleman, of the distinction between Kentish Men and Men of Kent and that you are still to the west of the River Medway. The River Bourne runs here, a tributary of the Medway and one with enough force to power the paper mills.

West Peckham

The Peckhams, East and West, have long recorded histories, each being named after the peak or summit on which they stand. You first pass by the old house of Hamptons, which had stood for centuries and was rebuilt in 1833. It has Ionic columns on the south eastern side, in the Palladian style then becoming popular.

Far more important in the story of the region was Oxen Hoath, home first to the old family of Colepeper from late Norman times. The present house was first built in the 17th and 18th centuries, then redesigned in 1813 for Sir William Geary, whose family had succeeded to the estate and whose interests focused a large collection of French furniture. He had the domed roof designed by the architect Anthony Salvin, in French Empire style.

Across the Green in West Peckham, St Dunstan's Church, built in ragstone and said to date from Saxon times, has many memorials both to the Colepepers and to the Gearys. Sir John Colepeper, a judge, founded a chapel in 1408 as a

chantry for daily prayers for Henry IV. This later became the private pew for the Geary family.

On the corner at the east of the village Duke's Place has stood since the 15th century. It stands on land granted by Sir John Colepeper to the Knights Hospitallers of the Order of St John in 1337. It may have been the local Commandery until the order was dissolved in 1540. The Order of the Knights

View of Royden Hall

Hospitallers was founded during the time of the Crusades to care for the sick and the wounded and to look after Christian pilgrims going to Jerusalem.

Old East Peckham

St Michael's Church now maintained by the Redundant Churches Fund, was left to stand

alone on its hill when East Peckham, drawn by the increasing trade on the Medway, moved in the late 18th century, to its present site beside the river. To the east of St Michael's Church at East Peckham lies Roydon Hall, once the home of Sir Roger Twysden, a keen Royalist and pamphleteer. At the beginning of the Civil War the 'knights of the shire of Kent' were moderate, almost Parliamentarian, but events moved them towards the Royalist cause. Sir Roger spent some time as a prisoner of the Parliamentarians in a hulk on the Thames. Roydon Hall is now the home of the international transcendental movement in England.

By the stile between Moat Wood and the arable fields, you

see the land gradually sloping down to the Medway valley. Carving its way between the Greensand hills, the River Medway, largest river in the South East, has played a crucial role in the history of the region. The Romans called it Meduwaeias, the Saxons Medwaeg, both basing the name of a Celtic word, 'Medu', meaning 'sweet water'.

River Medway

The Medway rises as a small spring in the Ashdown Forest near Turners Hill, then meanders from the High Weald through the Wealden plain. Among its tributaries is the River Eden. The Beult and Teise join it at Yalding. Often a gentle stream, after heavy rain the Medway can be a torrent pouring down from the clay slopes of the High Weald. Early on the fertile slopes attracted settlers. Neolithic long barrows have been found in several places. Bronze and Iron Age settlers were followed by the Romans whose large complex at Eccles is their most important in the region.

From the earliest days the river has been navigable on its tidal stretch almost as far as

Maidstone. The Romans transported ragstone from their quarries on the Greensand ridge, shipping it to the Thames and on to London for building. Corn and iron from the Weald was also transported. Towards the end of the 16th century the wealthy ironmasters and timber merchants to the south looked for better ways to move their goods. By Tudor times heavy canon and artillery, even more than fire-backs and domestic goods, were transported from the High Weald to the Thames and then to London.

First the ironmasters extended to the non-tidal stretch a campaign they had long waged to keep the river clear of fallen trees and fish weirs and made navigable a six-mile stretch from Maidstone to Yalding. Soon they looked to increasing navigation higher up the Medway. In 1627 a new commission was appointed to negotiate with land owners and so increase the transport of goods from the iron works of the

High Weald. Early in 1665 an Act was at last passed to ensure navigation to carry iron goods, ordnance, timber, corn, hops, wool, leather, coals, limestone and other commodities. But it was not until the mid-18th century that negotiations really succeeded. Another Act of 1740 authorised the efforts to make the Medway navigable as far as Forest Row.

Hampstead Lock, one of ten along the Upper Medway Navigation, and the canal at Yalding, constructed to provide a straighter stretch for traffic, result from those efforts. For over a 100 years first iron, then timber for the naval shipyards at Chatham, headed the list of

goods transported down the Medway.

Yalding

The low-lying land between the Medway and Yalding, known as The Lees, was created by alluvial deposits brought down by the river from the High Weald. The land used to flood regularly until a flood barrier above Tonbridge was created. Each of the ten locks between Leigh and Allington have flood control sluices, managed by the Environment Agency. Today the Lees is unimproved grassland and you will find bird's-foot-trefoil and lady's bedstraw growing with several other wild flowers.

High Street, Yalding

Yalding, a small town at the confluence of the Medway, Beult and Teise, and an important river crossing, is thought to take its name from the elders (Eold-ingas) who met there regularly in Saxon times. Its collection of old houses, attractive streets, the medieval bridges and St Peter's Church make it a worthwhile place to pause and explore. Cleave's Grammar School was founded and endowed by William Cleave, citizen and haberdasher of London, in 1663 as a free school in this parish for the teaching of reading, writing and arithmetic

Hunton

The slopes above Yalding to the east of the Medway are rich in hop gardens and orchards. Here you enter one of the most fertile areas in Kent for fruit of any kind.

Along the ridge the old manorial names linger on. The earliest recorded names giving a clue to their origin - Buston after de Byrston, Reason Hill after John de Reison. Houses such as Burston Manor and Barn Hill have long been marked on the maps. Land use has changed several times here.

In the time of Elizabeth I the slopes above Hunton came into the Despencer family who created parkland here. This reverted to farmland in the 19th century with small, enclosed fields. Today hardly a hedge remains. There has been a farm complex at Buston Manor for at least five centuries. The granary to the south, built of ragstone and with gables and red brick eaves, has stood since the late 16th century, the weather-boarded barn beyond it even longer.

In the complex of buildings at Barn Hill Farm, Weavers House stands out with its half-timbering and plaster infill. It is said to have been the home of a Flemish weaver in the 17th century.

Linton

Linton's distinctive houses on the east side of the main road were built in mock-Tudor style in the middle of the 19th century. They formed part of the estate which had grown up around Linton Park, home of the Mann family to whom monuments stand in St Nicholas' Church. Linton House, huge and impressive with white stucco, lies on the

scarp slope, overlooking its parkland. Thomas Mann first built it in the 1730s, in Palladian style, with two floors. Thomas Cubitt added a third in 1829.

The house had once been known as Capell Court, owned in the 17th century by Sir John Mayney who was created a baronet by Charles I. In the Civil War the house was surrounded by Cromwell's men. Sir John defended himself along with his retainers but the Roundheads rushed the

place and the house was sequestered. When the house was restored to Sir John he eventually sold it to the Mann family. One of the family, Horace Mann, was Ambassador to Rome in the 18th century. His correspondence with Horace Walpole lasted for 45 years and filled 42 volumes.

*Lychgate, Bou
Monchelsea C*

Boughton Monchelsea

Boughton Monchelsea Place is another house set in a dramatic position on the edge of the escarpment with views to Tenterden church, Goudhurst, Benenden and to the South Downs. On the slopes below lies its own park where fallow deer have wandered for 300 years.

The present ragstone house was built from 1567 onwards on the site of a mediaeval manor house. The battlements were installed in 1819. The name Boughton, pronounced Borton, comes from Bocton, meaning a clearing in a beech wood, Monchelsea from the Monchensies, a Norman family who held the land in the 12th century.

The first owner of the present house was Robert Rudston who went to the Tower of London for taking part in the rebellion of Thomas Wyatt, a friend of his, in 1554, just after he had bought the house. He bought the place back on his release and went on to complete his alterations. Continuously occupied since it was first built, the house still includes an Elizabethan staircase, a late 17th-century staircase, 18th-century mock Gothic pillars in the hall and a Regency dining room.

You will find the Church of St Peter to the south-west corner of the garden. Much of this was rebuilt in the 19th century after a fire in 1832, but further work in the 1870s re-used old Perpendicular windows and some traces of the original Norman church. The 16th-century lychgate, with roof supported by a crown post, may be the oldest in England. To the west of the lychgate is a mounting block whose top stone is dated 1717. In the churchyard is a unique collection of tombstones, showing the variety of ways people chose to remember their loved ones. They include a mausoleum, some table tombs, a line of body tombs and a headstone showing a man jumping out of his coffin at the sound of the last trump.

Chart Sutton

The small chartland parish of Chart Sutton has for centuries been at the centre of arable and fruit farming. Hops were grown at Chart Sutton in the 17th century, vines even earlier.

The region contains some good half-timbered houses dating from as early as the 15th century, such as Ladds Court on the hilltop and Hernden or Heronden below, owned originally by wealthy yeomen farmers. Beside St Michael's Church at Chart Sutton itself stands Chart Place, a fine Queen Anne house, built in 1708 for the Desbouverie family who had recently bought an estate in Folkestone. The farmhouse and granary just beyond were built at the same time with Wealden brick chequer work and with shaped end gables. When Jacob Desbouverie moved from London one of the attractions must surely have been the chance to farm in this prosperous area. The mounting block at the gate of St Michael's Church ensured a welcome for the more distant parishioners.

Sutton Valence

Sutton Valence, once held by the Valence family, has all the appearance of a small hill town, perched on the edge of the escarpment. Its terraced roads follow the contours of the hillside, largely untouched by the traffic which runs on the one-in-eight slope of the A274. The Greensand Way takes you past the front of the boys' school founded by William Lambe in 1576. A wealthy clothmaker, he is also remembered in Lamb's Conduit Street in Holborn, where he brought water to the area in 1577. Sutton Valence is rich in old buildings. Not to be missed are almshouses also founded by William Lambe in

Roses by a notice board, Sutton Valence

1580, in the High Street. Sutton Valence has always been a place of strategic importance. From Roman times at least two earlier roads met here from the south, one from the port at Lympne, the other from Rye. The Normans established a castle here whose ruins still stand, to guard the route to Rye. In St Mary's churchyard is the tombstone of John Willes (1777-1852), the cricketer who introduced round-arm bowling.

Chapter Six

THROUGH ORCHARDS TO SANDSTONE HEATH

Sutton Valence ~ Godinton Park

As you leave Sutton Valence you pass through East Sutton, scene of dramatic moments in the Civil War, then walk on to Ulcombe, where history and legend combine in its ancient church. At Boughton Malherbe you pass the mansion where Queen Elizabeth I visited the Wotton family, while at Pluckley, home of the Derings, come tales of daring escapes, as well as haunted houses. Little Chart still has a working mill but Little Chart Forstal is now a tranquil Green. The descent through Coldham Wood to Hothfield Common brings you to a National Nature Reserve, a wildlife haven with heath and bogs on a sandstone plateau.

East Sutton

Another area of quiet farmland, East Sutton, came into prominence through the Filmer family who moved in 1610 to East Sutton Place, now one of HM's Prisons. This had first been built in the late 16th century and you can see the original gables with their moulded finials beyond the tall, 19th-century walls. One of the Filmers, Sir Robert, was a friend of Charles II and one of the more extreme Royalists, an allegiance he displayed in his book 'Patriarcha' where he declared his support for the king by writing on the divine right of kings. He paid for this when General Fairfax besieged him in the house and subsequently imprisoned him in Leeds Castle. The house was forfeit but later restored to Sir Robert and his family.

East Sutton church, dedicated to St Peter and St Paul, was built mainly in the 13th century. The north wall, visible from the road, still has its original Perpendicular window with superb tracery. The church contains a number of memorials to the Filmer family.

The Filmers had moved from Otterden in the 16th century, presumably in search of more land to farm and of the view that was now becoming so valued. Their first house was Charlton Court, below the Way, on the steep slope of the combe to the south-east. This was mainly built in brick, laid in English bond, in 1612 . You can see elaborate gables which date from this time though much else were later additions.

Farming practice

The 17th century was one of considerable agricultural expansion throughout Kent. The Filmer farm at East Sutton provided fascinating records of farming practice, which shows a mixed farm of pasture, arable, hops and apples. In 1740 the Filmer estates here and elsewhere in Kent were valued at £1,620.15s.

Hops are still grown on the fertile slopes of the combe. Today they are much reduced in number. Though now much automated, hop-growing is still labour-intensive. The traditional seasonal activities continue - stringing in spring, with a long pole, twiddling in early summer as well as harvesting in early September.

Hothfield Common

Bell House, Boughton Malherbe

The church, one of several on an old pilgrim route along the ridge, leading to Canterbury, is unusually large for its setting, as a College of Priests was established here by Archbishop Stephen Langton between 1213 and 1215, at the petition of Ralph St Leger. Look for the five carved misericords which are assumed to be those of the five priests of the college. Look also for the fine brasses in the north chapel of some of the St Leger family and for the mediaeval wall paintings, especially those in the south aisle. One shows Dives and Lazarus; the other shows the Devil and St Michael weighing souls. The yew tree near the entrance is thought to be at least one thousand years old. Recent research suggests it may be much older still, rumour claiming three to be nearer the mark. Ulcombe village is lower down the ridge, The Harrow Inn just half a mile away, is worth a detour if you do not mind the uphill return journey.

You can see signs of the busier days on either side of the combe. Beside the road on the west stands one of the best oast houses of its kind, built in chequered red brick and weatherboarded above. On the other side of this valley you will see converted hoppers huts, originally set up to house the temporary hop pickers, many of whom came from the East End of London for the hop picking season.

Ulcombe

At Ulcombe you can see the now-familiar red and grey brick on part of the ground floor of the gable end of 17th-century Church Farmhouse Here the bricks were laid in Flemish bond. Mathematical tiles cover most of the front elevation. Ulcombe, meaning the valley of the owl, used to be pronounced Ookem or Uckham. In Domesday Book it boasted a church and one mill. Legend about the local St Leger family, whose family kept close connection with it for over 700 years, adds colour, for Sir Robert de St Leger who came with William the Conqueror not only helped William to land on the beach near Hastings but also, so the story goes, killed a 'pagan Dane' at Ulcombe. Also according to legend, William the Conqueror himself stood on the site of the ragstone church at Ulcombe and gave orders for its building.

Certainly of Norman origin as you can see from the outlines of two Norman windows in the north wall of the nave, the Church of All Saints has acquired additions over the years, with an Early English sanctuary, a 14th-century chancel and tower and a Decorated lady chapel.

Boughton Malherbe

Boughton Malherbe, so named because one Robert de Malherbe held the manor at the time of King John, is one of the smallest villages on the Greensand Way, with a farm and a few houses centred on the Church of St Nicholas. What you see in the attractive ragstone Boughton Place with its mullioned windows is the one surviving wing of a much larger house built in the late 16th century by Sir Edward Wotton. Farm buildings to the south were first erected around his time. Sir Edward enlarged and improved the house in readiness for a visit by Queen Elizabeth I. In return she invited him to be a courtier but he refused at first, conscious of the cost of keeping a London residence. By 1630 Boughton Place was one of the most extensive estates in the county, more compact but almost as large as the Canterbury lands.

Boughton Place is perhaps best known for Sir Edward's son, Sir Henry Wotton, who was born here in 1568. He took Holy Orders, was Provost of Eton and later became a Diplomat going first to the Court of James VI of Scotland where he was knighted.

Famous for his aphorism 'An Ambassador is an honest man, sent to lie abroad for the good of his country'; he later became ambassador to the Court of Venice. His interests were wide-ranging for, in addition to writing a book on 'The Elements of Architecture', he was also a poet. He wrote 'On his mistress, the Queen of Bohemia' ('You meaner beauties of the night.'). He had a fine library and today his books are collectors items.

The ragstone Church of St Nicholas was another on the old pilgrim route to Canterbury. It is Decorated in style but was refitted in the 19th century. Naturally enough, it contains numerous Wotton monuments, though none, it would seem, to Sir Henry. It contains a beautiful pulpit with linenfold panelling. The yew tree was planted at the time Queen Elizabeth came to visit.

To the south lies Coldbridge Farm, one of the best of the many moated houses of medieval times. Here in the very early 13th century, one Fulk de Pehforer threw a moat around his manor house to defend himself from the very real threat of his

enemies. He also built a fishpond to provide food for himself, his family and retainers and enclosed his animals within a paddock.

The surrounding slopes and the land where the route drops to the spring line have been farmed over many centuries. Burscombe Farm on the far slope was built in the 18th century or earlier. Hollis Farmhouse may even date from the 14th century. But land use has changed considerably. Maps from the last century show small, enclosed fields. Now the hedges have gone and today you will see a mixture of practices, set-aside, pasture and arable.

Egerton

The Decorated tower of St James Church, Egerton, visible from miles around, is another much restored in Victorian times. If it is open, look for the huge, 18th-century three-tiered chandelier which hangs from a cherub's head. The altar rail, showing St Thomas a Becket, St Augustine and other saints kneeling to support it, was made in 1958.

The Street contains a number of interesting old buildings. Church House was a medieval hall house but refaced with brick. The Bakery dates from the 17th century, while on the corner stands The George Inn, 18th century, with weatherboarding and tiled roof.

Harvesting near Pluckley

Pluckley

Pluckley has become well known for its small square outside The Black Horse, filmed for H.E.Bates' 'The Darling Buds of May', but it also has another claim to fame. Ranking as the most haunted village in a county which already passes the national average for ghostly appearances, it boasts a phantom coach and horses, a highwayman who died in a fight and a Red Lady who grieves in the churchyard.

The village has a long history. The Church of St Nicholas, with its ragstone walls and shingled spire has been here since the 13th century. Normans and Saxons were here before then. Inside the church are two fine screens, known as parclose screens. A Tudor screen, dating from 1475, stands between the chancel and the chapel. With foliage in late Perpendicular style this is very similar to another in Ulcombe church. The other screen at Pluckley, at the chapel entrance, was built later, in 1635, with Ionic columns in Classical revival style.

Brass plaques recall members of the Dering family between 1425 to 1610. The people were real enough but the brasses seem to have been faked in the 17th century by Sir Edward Dering, when making alterations to the church, to enhance his family reputation. It is by a less usual memorial that Sir Edward himself is remembered. A distinguished member of parliament and man of letters, and another Kent supporter of King Charles I, he is said to have escaped from his Roundhead pursuers by jumping out of a window with a relieving arch tall enough for him to do so because it was arched.

This arch became a motif for the houses built on Dering land. A descendent of Sir Edward, Sir Edward Cholmely Dering, had the local houses built in the 19th century in identical style, all with a low arch to their windows. You will find the windows all the same, the 'lucky' windows of Pluckley, two arched lights under a depressed relieving arch. Born in 1807, Sir Edward Cholmeley Dering started his building career at an early age for Sheerland House, the home farm of the estate, was built by him in 1813.

Surrenden Dering

The Dering home was at Surrenden Dering, built by the earlier Sir Edward in 1630, in the centre of the parish above the scarp, in what was regarded as an elegant situation, in a park 'beautifully clothed with timber and rich pastures'. It was noted for its shaped gables, similar to those at Knole and at Godinton.

Pluckley

Sadly, Dering 'lucky' windows installed in the 19th century failed to save much of the house from fire in 1952. The stabling with its high arch and pedimental gable dates from 18th century.

Little Chart

Little Chart lies in a valley where the Great Stour opens into old mill ponds. A modern mill continues the tradition of paper-making, started here in 1771. Nearby the ford was already in use in Roman times. The Swan has been standing since the 15th century, but with Dering windows added in the 19th century. St Mary's Church was built in 1955 to replace the medieval church which was bombed in the Second World War and considered too damaged for repair. The ruins of the old church, which include a Perpendicular tower, stand two-thirds of a mile to the north-west.

Little Chart Forstal

The Great Stour flows eastwards to Ashford, then north through Canterbury, to reach the sea at Sandwich. Little Chart Forstal, known in the past variously as Broken Fostal and even Brokett

Fostel, is set around a Green on higher ground above the Stour. The name 'Forstal' means land in front of a farm building. Surrounding the Green you will see a variety of houses dating from the 17th and 18th centuries, all conserved and restored from days when this was a small working, farming community. From 1931 until his death in 1974, H.E. Bates lived at The Granary, which he and his wife had converted from an old barn.

Hothfield Common

Hothfield Common lies on a sandy plateau, formed from an outcrop of the Folkestone Sands. This rests on clay which, being impermeable, forces water to resurface as acid springs. These waterlogged conditions have led to the slow build up of peat bogs where you will find a variety of plants, some of them particularly colourful, such as cotton grass, bog asphodel, marsh St John's wort and sundew. Twelve varieties of sphagnum moss have been found here, including two for which this is the only known locality in Kent. You will see dragonflies, especially the powder blue blue-keeled skimmer.

The Common itself used to provide land for all to use, with the chance to keep a cow and poultry and the opportunity to dig for peat in the bogs. It was well used as such and attracted people in some numbers to live here. This benefited the heathland habitat and created a patchwork of heather-dominated heathland or acidic grassland. When grazing ceased

Hothfield bog

in 1940 these ancient habitats, fashioned over centuries, began to deteriorate. Bracken took over and trees, no longer felled regularly, began to encroach. Today Hothfield Common is a National Nature Reserve managed by Kent Wildlife Trust and English Nature. Together these organisations actively manage the Common to conserve it, felling the trees which encroach, bulldozing away the bracken then mowing

back new growth on the heathland. Cattle graze again and you may even see Shetland ponies. In the bogs the birch and sallow which have invaded are being removed to bring light into the area.

All this has reintroduced to the area a rich variety of wildlife. The heather has returned to the Common and with it have

come moths, bees, wasps and ants. The bog is seeing its plant life restored. In addition the wood-land supports a range of breeding birds, including wood-peckers, treecreepers and tree pipit, while in a pond formed on the western side all three British species of newt have been found breeding. On Foxenhill Toll to the north-east stands an old plantation established in the 19th century with beech and Scots pine.

Chapter Seven

OLD TOWNS AND ANCIENT WOODLANDS
Godinton Park ~ Hamstreet

On the last stages of the walk old estates still figure, first at Hothfield where the land once belonged to the Earls of Thanet, then at Godinton where house and parkland were owned by the Toke family. Great Chart stands on a hill, long ago a thriving small town in its own right, now a village along one main street. The Way then leads you over arable and pasture on the lower slopes of the Greensand ridge. Ham Street Woods offer another priceless nature reserve. Hamstreet itself lies at the end of the Way, quiet again now that a new road has removed the traffic. Its tales of smuggling suggest that life was once not as quiet as had been thought.

Hothfield

The village of Hothfield stands on higher ground above the heath itself where the land attracted those who could afford it for its healthier fertile pastures. The land was long owned by the Tuftons who rose in status in the time of Charles I and soon became Earls of Thanet. Their name is recalled by the 'Thanet Arms' and in a few surviving aspects of the old estate.

The clearest evidence lies in the strong brick, buttressed walls, designed by James Wyatt, which surround the old parkland of Hothfield Place. This mansion stood to the west of the church, surrounded by trees, a square building built in the Portland stone that came to be desired as a building material in the 19th century. Hothfield Place replaced an earlier house built in the time of Elizabeth I but pulled down in 1954. Only an old stable block remains, now converted into modern homes.

The Tuftons did much for St Margaret's Church, noticeable for the slender shingled spike which rises from a Decorated tower. Inside is a monument to Sir John Tufton who died in 1624. He rebuilt the church in 1598, some years after lightning had struck down the original. This explains the late-Perpendicular windows which gave much more light than windows of an earlier date. It also explains why Sir John received such a magnificent monument, having a sea lion at his feet, a lion's paw at his wife's feet and family all around.

Chestnut coppicing in Ham Street Woods

In Hothfield churchyard beside a yew tree next to the path is a headstone to one Sarah Stanford who of died of smallpox in 1790.

On it is the epitaph:

'Her soul without a spot is gone to heaven;
Her spotted body to the worms is given.'

Below the church you have the choice of two routes. Both lead to Great Chart, one across low-lying water meadows before a last climb to Great Chart, the other through Godinton Park.

Godinton

Godinton was always a much smaller estate than those of Surrenden Dering and Hothfield but it has survived in a way that neither of the other two have managed. Not only does Godinton House still stand but it is maintained as a private home, and is on view from time to time to the public. The parkland too has been preserved.

Godinton, once the town of Godda's folk, was known as Goddington in the 13th century. At some point in the next century Simon de Godinton built a house here for his family, but the family most associated with Godinton is that of the Tokes, said to have been descended from Le Sieure de Touque who fought at the Battle of Hastings. The Tokes acquired the manor in the 15th century.

The best known of the Tokes was Captain Nicholas who inherited in 1627. He immediately rebuilt the medieval house, as the date 1628 on drain pipes clearly shows. The central hall and some of the old roof timbers still remain, but it is a 17th-century house, in brick, with

shaped gables, similar to those introduced at Knole in 1605, which now recalls a family who remained here for 400 years. The house stands in the middle of the park, over a rise, a little to the south of the Greensand Way. Its interior is especially renowned for its intricately carved woodwork and for its fireplace of Bethersden marble.

Great Chart

Chart Avenue led from Godinton to Great Chart, still recorded as Chart Magna in the 1801 Ordnance Survey map. Today Great Chart shows little sign that once it was more important than Ashford, with a second main street to the east flanked with houses. Marauding Danes burned Great Chart to

Godinton Park

the ground in the ninth century and, in its turn, Ashford grew in importance beside a crossing over the Stour. It is said a market house once stood in the field beside the church. That had gone by the 1790s when Hasted wrote his ´History of Kent', but a weekly market and a yearly fair on Lady day, first granted by Henry VI, were still held.

Most of Great Chart lies on the one street, where you will see shaped gables on the almshouses, built in 1833, and on the school, built in 1835. Both were built by the Tokes. The Church of St Mary the Virgin stands on higher ground at the top of the main street, a fine landmark with its late 14th-century ragstone tower visible from far and wide. There are traces of an earlier, Norman church, built in stone from Caen in Normandy. The 14th-century builders also used some stone from the Roman road which ran just south of Great Chart.

The church contains some fine memorials, tablets and brasses. The Toke family owned the north chapel and you should look if you can for memorials to various of their number. Stories abound but the most intriguing is that of Nicholas Toke who died in 1680. Now remembered in brass on the floor, with five wives and three daughters, tradition has it there might have been a sixth wife had he not died while travelling to London to seek her. He was 93 at the time. His longevity was attributed to the healthy air.

The 15th-century building at the gate is known as the Pest House, but such a place would not have been so close to the church. More likely it was a meeting place, or perhaps a priest's house. Further west lies Court Lodge, built of stone in 1313, once a manor house of Christ Church Priory at Canterbury, whose land this was. The land had been given to the monks in 799, for sheep rearing, to help to provide their clothing.

From the top of the hill by the limestone quarry now in-filled, to the south-east of Great Chart, you can see the flood plain of the Great Stour to the north. Still only a small river, it belies its former self, for once the entire valley was estuary until alluvium silted up to give the present fertile land. On the North Downs beyond you can

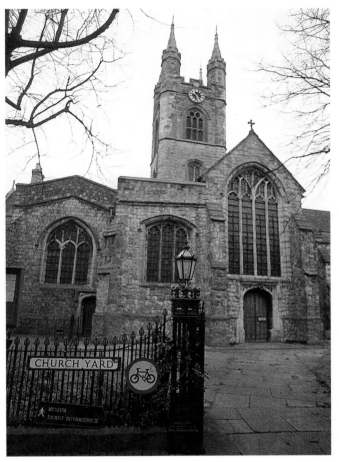

Ashford church

see clearly the route of the Pilgrims Way running below the tree line.

At the top of Mock Lane you have a chance for another view, this time southwards. The slopes dropping downhill ahead were once old cliffs. Beyond lies Romney Marsh, once a

huge bay. The cliff line was still very clear even in Roman times but upward movement of the sea bed was already producing small islands in the bay. Longshore drift along the coast gradually created a shingle bank which all but enclosed the area. Meanwhile alluvial deposit from the River Rother was

accumulating. In the Middle Ages the process of 'inning' the marshes, that is enclosing large areas and draining them, slowly but steadily converted swamp into pasture. Now, fully drained, Romney Marsh forms an area used largely for sheep grazing and wheat production.

Kingsnorth

Kingsnorth, once known as Kinges-snode, stretches along the slope of a rise which looks north towards Ashford. Most of the village has grown up in the last century. Only a few buildings having stood for longer. Beside the road is the 18th-century Queens Head. On the top of the hill is the late 14th-century Church of St Michael and All Angels. It is relatively small, with few decorations but has attractive stained glass windows from the 15th century, one window showing St Michael himself. Diminutive, weather-boarded Mouse Hall, beside the church gate, was first built in the 15th century, perhaps in similar style to the building outside the church at Great Chart.

You now come to a stretch of rolling agricultural land where

Hythe Beds sink below the surface and the Greensand ridge levels out into broad fields. Edward Hasted, who had a horror of flat land in general, described the area as 'flat and dreary'. He did not like the roads which he considered wide, with their dense hedgerows overhung by oaks. Today faster roads have replaced those which were 'miry and impassable' for much of the year, but the scattered farms and buildings, well-conserved, at Chilmington Green and at Willowbed Farmhouse, between Great Chart and Kingsnorth, and Bond and Taylor Farmhouse further south, all record the communities of 200 years ago. Reminders of still earlier times are seen in the moated houses at Singleton Manor to the east of Great Chart, Great Chilmington beside the Greensand Way and Court Lodge Farm.

Woodland management

Ham Street Woods is all that remains in this area of the great forest which developed after the last Ice Age. The fine woodland consists mainly of oak, but there are many other trees growing such as hawthorn,

the wild service tree and aspen and willow. The wood has been managed as a National Nature Reserve since 1953 by English Nature. Some parts are maintained as high forest, other parts coppiced, while the 'traditional coppice with standards' contains a mixture handed down by generations. In this way the woods provide valuable habitats for all kinds of wildlife. Some areas of the woods are kept as high forest. As well as the predominant tall standard oaks which provide a canopy for dense undergrowth there are also birch, cherry, rowan, field maple and ash. These standard trees are home to numerous birds, including the tawny owl, woodpeckers, nut-hatch, hawfinch and treecreepers.

Other areas are coppiced on a 15 to 20-year rotation, following the traditional methods carried out for centuries. Here hornbeam and chestnut predominate. The

Path above Golden Wood

coppicing leads to another kind of habitat and so benefits a different range of wildlife. In the first few years after the wood has been cut there is a flush of wild flowers as light and air penetrate the undergrowth. After that, between four to ten years after coppicing, the thick regrowth provides the ideal habitat for breeding birds. Ham Street Woods are especially known for the warblers and, above all, the nightingales which abound in these conditions.

Other areas again are kept as wide, open rides. Moths and

butterflies thrive in the more open areas of the wood, such as merveille du-jour or light orange underwing, and there are many dragonflies. Here in spring you will find wood anemones, bluebells and violets. In some parts a different system altogether prevails, one of total non-intervention except for recording of development.

The woods were severely damaged by the 1987 storm. Even ten years on it is too early to see the effects but as dead wood accumulates so the habitat improves. You should stay on the official rights of way, not only for the sake of the wildlife but also to avoid danger from rotten limbs of trees.

Hamstreet

Once Hamstreet village, a small hamlet within the parish of Orlestone, consisted of only a few houses. One of these houses would have been the converted Wealden hall house beside the cross roads. Its only church, the Wesleyan Chapel, was built in 1872 on whose site John Wesley had earlier preached. The railway, built in 1851, led to some 19th-century growth but most development has occurred more recently.

With roads deep in mud and impassable for much of the year, it must have been isolated from much that happened to the north. Even so, links were kept. The Earls of Thanet, from Hothfield, owned land here and encouraged an annual fair on land nearby. In the 18th and 19th centuries The Duke's Head became a favourite haunt of smugglers such as the Butchers and the Ransleys. These notorious gangs who frequented Romney Marsh used Hamstreet as a route to take their goods to higher ground. This may have had some benefits to local people who from time to time discovered small hoards, presumably hidden in a hurry, such as an oak box found under a hedge containing silver spoons and lace, or an old jar of coins ploughed up in a field near kilns above the railway station.

Royal Military Canal

To the south of Hamstreet lies the Royal Military Canal which runs across the Marsh from Hythe to Cliff End near Fairlight. This was built between 1804 and 1809 as part of the nation's defences in case of invasion by

Napoleon. It was also intended that it would catch water from the higher ground and so relieve flooding on the marsh. It would, it was hoped, also help in the transport of shingle from the beaches for road making.

There was even a scheme to link the canal with a proposed network of canals throughout Kent, so opening the interior of the county via Chatham, Rye and Hythe to the sea. While the canal's defensive capacity was never put to the test and the Kent canal scheme never materialised, the canal provided a useful means of transport across the marsh for over a century. Today the Royal Military Canal is classed as an Ancient Monument. Its waterways are an SSSI.

As you followed the route along the Greensand ridge you will have noticed a number of changes in land use along the way. Woodland has vanished or in some cases returned. Industry has come and gone. Open countryside has changed to parkland, then become farmland in due course. Orchards and hop gardens have flourished, then disappeared, only to be planted once again.

Hamstreet was the choice for a series of stamps, issued in 1991 to mark the bi-centenary of the Ordnance Survey as the official mapping agency for Great Britain. These show the village as depicted in Ordnance Survey maps published during the last two centuries. They show the development of cartography and also reveal some of the major changes that have come to the area.

The first stamp (24p) shows the 1816 edition of the 1801 map of Kent, which was hand-engraved on copper plates. The Royal Military Canal, recently completed, appears in the bottom right hand corner. The second stamp (28p) shows the 1906 map, with increasingly complex symbols, such as contour lines, and also woodlands. In addition it shows the railway which had been completed in 1851.

The third stamp (33p) shows the 1959 map, now bearing symbols for electricity lines. Here you can also see

the chapel and the post office. The fourth stamp (39p) shows the 1991 edition of the Ordnance Survey map. This time you find additional details such as the new symbol for orchards, and the change in road colouring – red for A roads, brown for B roads etc. The Saxon Shore Way long-distance path appears on this stamp for the first time. The stamps summarise the importance of Ordnance Survey maps not only as guides to the countryside but as a record of social and economic development.

Reproduced by permission of the Post Office

65

View of Bough Beech Reservoir from Hanging Bank

Greensand Ridge

EXPLORING THE AREA

Interesting places to visit on or near the Greensand Way

Haslemere Museum
78 High Street, Haslemere
Tel: (01428) 642112

Oakhurst Cottage
(by appointment only)
Hambledon, Nr Godalming
Tel: (01428) 683207

Leith Hill Tower
Nr Coldharbour, Dorking
Tel: (01306) 711777

Goddards
Abinger Common,
Dorking
Tel: (01628) 825920

Dorking and District Museum
62a West Street, Dorking
Tel: (01306) 743821

The Windmill Church
Reigate Heath, Reigate
Tel: (01737) 221100

Denbies Wine Estate
London Road, Dorking
Tel: (01306) 876616

Reigate Priory Museum
c/o Reigate Priory Junior
School, Bell Street, Reigate
Tel: (01737) 245065

Squerryes Court
Westerham
Tel: (01959) 562345

Quebec House
Westerham
Tel: (01892) 890651

Chartwell
Westerham
Tel: (01732) 866368

Riverhill House Gardens
Sevenoaks
Tel: (01732) 458802/452557

Knole
Sevenoaks
Tel: (01732) 450608/462100

**Sevenoaks Museum
and Art Gallery**
Buckhurst Lane, Sevenoaks
Tel: (01732) 453118

Black Charles
Underriver, Nr Sevenoaks
Tel: (01732) 833036

Ightham Mote
Ivy Hatch, Sevenoaks
Tel: (01732) 810378

Old Soar Manor
Plaxtol, Borough Green
Tel: (01732) 810378

Boughton Monchelsea Place
Boughton Monchelsea,
Nr Maidstone
Tel: (01622) 743120

Sutton Valence Castle
Sutton Valence, Nr Maidstone

Godinton House
Godinton Park, Ashford
Tel: (01233) 612669

Parish churches – en route
(keys usually obtained locally if
not open)

Village pump, Brockham

Countryside open spaces
on or near the Greensand Way

Hindhead Common, Devil's
Punch Bowl and Gibbet Hill

Thursley Common

Witley Common

Hydons Heath

Winkworth Arboretum
Hascombe Road, Godalming
Tel: (02483) 308477

Winterfold Heath

Pitch Hill

Holmbury Hill

Leith Hill and Wotton Common

The Nower

Reigate Heath

Reigate Priory Park

Redhill Common

Tiburstow Hill

Limpsfield Common

The High Chart
Limpsfield

Crockhamhill Common

Toy's Hill

Ide Hill

Bough Beech Reservoir
(by permit only)
Tel: (01622) 662012

Emmetts Garden
Ide Hill, Nr Sevenoaks
Tel: (01732) 750367

Hanging Bank and
Brockhoult Mount

Knole Park
(open to pedestrians by courtesy
of Lord Sackville)

One Tree Hill

Shipbourne Common

Dene Park
Shipbourne

Yalding Lees

Hothfield Common
Tel: (01622) 662012

Ham Street Woods
Tel: (01233) 812525

For further information and
details about most of these
countryside open spaces in Surrey
and Kent, please telephone (0181)
541 9463 and (01622) 696411
respectively.

Other walking opportunities

If you have enjoyed this walk and would like to explore other waymarked walking routes in Surrey and Kent, write to either the Rights of Way Unit, Marketing and Communications, Environment, Surrey County Council or the Access and Recreation Officer, Planning Department, Kent County Council for further information.

It is possible for you to devise your own shorter linear and circular walks using the extensive rights of way network throughout the counties. Information about these can be obtained by studying either the Ordnance Survey Explorer maps or the Surrey and Kent County Council's Definitive Maps of Public Rights of Way. Copies of the latter can be inspected at public libraries or district council offices. In the event of difficulty please contact the Rights of Way Units in either Surrey or Kent County Council offices.

Ted's seat, Golden Wood

Linked, or running close, to the Greensand Way are a number of other walks, as follows:

North Downs Way

Valued for its dramatic south-facing escarpment, secluded dry valleys, network of tiny lanes, isolated farms and churches, the North Downs are the backbone of the Surrey and Kent landscape rising between the capital and coast, seen by millions using the railways and motor-ways which skirt the boundaries.

Ancient woods, unimproved grasslands, scattered oast houses and small orchards provide a rich tapestry of wildlife habitats of international nature conserv-ation importance and a legacy of sites of historic interest.

The North Downs Way National Trail explores this special landscape along 153 miles of waymarked paths linking Farnham in Surrey to the White Cliffs of Dover.

Publications:

North Downs Way National Trail Guide - Neil Curtis, Aurum Press, 25 Bedford Avenue, London WC1B 3AT.

North Downs Way - A Users' Handbook - Kent County Council, Planning Department, Springfield, Maidstone, Kent ME14 2LX.

Wey-South Path

From Guildford the Path follows the towpath of the Godalming Navigation (this is part of the canalised River Wey, a tributary of the Thames) to its junction with the Wey-Arun Canal.

From here it follows the old towpath or farmland and woodland paths as near as possible to the line of the Wey-Arun Canal to meet the River Arun. Short sections of the canal have been restored, but in places it has been almost completely obliterated. The Path is 36 miles long.

The canal was last used as a waterway link between the Thames and the south coast in 1871.

Publication:

Wey-South Path - Aeneas Mackintosh, Wey and Arun Canal Trust Ltd, 24 Griffiths Avenue, Lancing, West Sussex BN15 0HW.

Downs Link

Running for 30 miles between two national trails, this is a north-south bridleway link which was developed by Surrey and West Sussex County Councils. From St Martha's Hill on the North Downs Way the Link follows bridleways over wooded heath and farmland to meet and follow the trackbed of the former Horsham and Guildford direct railway through Cranleigh to Christ's Hospital near Itchingfield. Here the trackbed of the former Shoreham to Itchingfield

Junction line is followed through Partridge Green and Bramber, crossing farmland to meet the South Downs Way.

Publications:

Downs Link Route Guide - West Sussex County Council, Planning Department, County Hall, Tower Street, Chichester, West Sussex PO19 1RL.

The South Downs Way and Downs Link - Kev Reynolds, Cicerone Press, 2 Police Square, Milnthorpe, Cumbria LA7 7PY.

Vanguard Way

The 63-mile Way, developed by Vanguards Rambling Club to lead from the suburbs of London to the sea, heads south-east from Croydon and crosses Selsdon Nature Reserve and the North Downs to Crockham Hill and Forest Row. From here it continues across the High Weald and through the woods and heaths of Ashdown Forest to Blackboys and Alfriston. It then crosses the South Downs to Exceat and follows the coast to Seaford, with an extension to Newhaven.

Publication:

The Vanguard Way - Colin Saunders, Vanguards Rambling Club, c/o 109 Selsdon Park Road, Croydon, CR2 8JJ.

Wealdway and Vanguard Way - Kev Reynolds, Cicerone Press, 2 Police Square, Milnthorpe, Cumbria LA7 7PY.

Wealdway

The Wealdway (80 miles) is an attractive scenic route across south-east England from the Thames estuary, over the North Downs and the Weald to the English Channel at Beachy Head. The route starts in Kent at the historic port of Gravesend and continues through Cobham with its associations with Charles Dickens, and over the dry valleys of the North Downs to the River Medway and Tonbridge. The route continues across the Weald and on through Ashdown Forest to Eastbourne at the foot of the South Downs.

The Wealdway is an interesting route with new major towns or settlements and gives many the opportunity to enjoy an unspoilt part of the South East.

St Peter's Church, Hambledon

Publications:

Wealdway - Geoffrey King, Wealdway Steering Group, c/o Dr Ben Perkins, 11 Old London Road, Brighton, Sussex BN1 8XR.

Wealdway Accommodation Guide - Wealdway Steering Group (address as above)

Wealdway and the Vanguard Way - Kev Reynolds, Cicerone Press, 1 Police Square, Milnthorpe, Cumbria LA7 7PY.

Medway Valley Walk

The Medway Valley Walk is a valley walk in west Kent between the historic town of Tonbridge and the cathedral city of Rochester.

The 28-mile route is of interest for its landscape and natural history, for its history and archaeology and riverain features.

The walk passes through a varied landscape of downland, woodland, orchards and hop gardens; meadows and farmland; lakes and marshland; unspoilt villages and historic towns. Linking all these features is the meandering River Medway.

Publication:

Medway Valley Walk - Kev Reynolds, Kent County Council, Planning Department, Springfield, Maidstone, Kent ME14 2LX.

Bridge near Hothfield bog

Roadside bouquet

Stour Valley Walk

A walk across east Kent along the valley of the River Stour from the source of the river at Lenham to the sea at Pegwell Bay. Passing through a varied but consistently attractive landscape, this 51½-mile route takes in downland, woodland, orchards, hop gardens, lakes, dykes and marshland, unspoilt villages and historic towns.

Between Lenham and Ashford the route passes through fertile farmland, Hothfield Common and Victoria Park. North of Ashford, the walker has an inviting prospect of the North Downs to the north. The route continues through a gap in the downs.

Further on, the City of Canterbury is a worthwhile stop for its places of historic and archaeological interest. East of Canterbury is Fordwich, the limit, in medieval times, of the navigable section of the river.

The remainder of the route traces the old Saxon shoreline of the Wantsum Channel to the important Roman site at Richborough, thence to the ancient Cinque Port of Sandwich, and the sea at Pegwell Bay.

Publication:

Stour Valley Walk - Veronica Litten, Kent County Council, Planning Department, Springfield, Maidstone, Kent ME14 2LX.

Saxon Shore Way

The Saxon Shore Way, running for 163 miles from Gravesend in Kent round the ancient coastline to Hastings in East Sussex, offers the long-distance walker an unrivalled diversity of scenery. The Way follows the wide expanses of marshland bordering the Thames and Medway estuaries and the White Cliffs of Dover. There are panoramic views over Romney Marsh from the escarpment that marks the ancient coastline between Folkestone and Rye, and from the sandstone cliffs of the High Weald at Hastings.

The route is also rich in historical sites and literary associations. Here the Romans invaded Britain and, later, built the 'Saxon Shore' forts to defend the island against a new wave of invaders. Here St Augustine landed to bring the Gospel to the Anglo-Saxon Kingdom which would later all to the Normans who, in their turn, erected great fortresses like Dover Castle to defend their conquests.

Publication:

Saxon Shore Way - Bea Cowan, Aurum Press, 25 Bedford Avenue, London WC1B 3AT or Kent County Council, Planning Department, Springfield, Maidstone, Kent ME14 2LX.

Other walking opportunities in the area

FURTHER INFORMATION

AND REFERENCES

Bibliography

Batsford Guide to the Industrial Archaeology of South East England (The)
A J Haselfoot
Batsford

Buildings of England (The): North East and East Kent
J Newman
Penguin Books

Buildings of England (The): Surrey
Bridget Cherry
Penguin Books

Buildings of England (The): West Kent and the Weald
J Newman
Penguin Books

Canals of South and South East England (The)
Charles Hadfield
David and Charles

Guide to the Industrial Archaeology of Surrey (A)
Glenys Crocker
Association for Industrial Archaeology

Guide to the Industrial History of Mole Valley District (A)
Peter Tarplee
Surrey Industrial History Group

Guide to the Industrial History of Tandridge (A)
Malcolm Tadd
Surrey Industrial History Group

History and Topographical Survey of the County of Kent (1797–1801) (The)
Edward Hasted
E P Publishing

History of Kent (A)
F W Jessup
Phillimore

History of Surrey (A)
Peter Brandon
Phillimore

Kent and East Sussex Waterways
P A L Vine
Middleton Press

Kent Houses
Anthony Quiney
Antique Collectors Club Ltd

Ordnance Survey Historical Guides: Kent
Felix Hull
George Philip/Ordnance Survey

Regional History of the South East from AD 1000 (A)
Peter Brandon and Brian Short
Longman

Roman Ways in the Weald
Ivan Margary
Phoenix House

Surrey
John Drewett
Shire

South-East England
Ronald Jessup
Thames and Hudson

Surrey: A County History
John Janaway
Countryside Books

Villages of Surrey (The)
Andy William and Graham Collyer
Countryside Books

Weald (The)
Wes Gibbons
Unwin Paperbacks

Weald (The)
S W Wooldridge and Frederick Goldring
Collins

Windmills of England
R J Brown
Robert Hale

Woodland Archaeology in Surrey: Its Recognition and Management
Nicola Bannister
Surrey County Council

Inn sign (listed monument), 'The White Hart', Bletchingly

Table of Historical Periods

Mesolithic	10000	–	3500BC	Prehistoric
Neolithic	3500	–	2000BC	
Bronze Age	2000	–	800BC	
Iron Age	800BC	–	AD43	
Roman	43	–	410	
Anglo-Saxon	410	–	1066	
Norman	1066	–	1154	
Plantagenets	1154	–	1399	Medieval
Lancastrians	1399	–	1461	
Yorkists	1461	–	1485	
Tudors	1485	–	1603	Renaissance
Elizabethan 1558	–	1603		
Stuarts	1603	–	1714	
Jacobean 1603	–	1649		
Commonwealth 1649	–	1660		
Restoration 1660	–	1702		
Anne 1702	–	1714		
Hanoverian	1714	–	1901	
Georgian 1714	–	1837		
Regency 1810	–	1820		
Victorian 1837	–	1901		
Edwardian	1901	–	1910	
Windsor	1910	–	Present day	

Table of Architectural Periods

Romanesque	1066	–	1190	
Early English	1190	–	1280	Gothic
Decorated	1280	–	1380	
Perpendicular	1380	–	1550	
Classical	1550	–	1810	
Gothic &				
Classical Revivals	1810	–	1914	
Modern	1914	–	Present day	

Countryside Access Charter

Your rights of way are:
▪ Public footpaths - on foot only.
▪ Bridleways - on foot, horseback and pedal cycle.
▪ Byways - (usually old roads), most roads used as public paths and public roads - all traffic.
Use maps, signs and waymarks. Ordnance Survey Explorer, Pathfinder and Landranger maps show most public rights of way.

On rights of way you can:
▪ Take a pram, pushchair or wheelchair if practicable.
▪ Take a dog (on a lead or under close control).
▪ Take a short route round an illegal obstruction or remove it sufficiently to get past.

You have a right to go for recreation to:
▪ Public parks and open spaces on foot.
▪ Most commons near older towns and cities - on foot and sometimes on horseback.
▪ Private land where the owner has a formal agreement with the local authority.

View looking south, over the Weald

In addition you can use the following by established or local custom or consent:
▪ Many areas of open country like moorland, fell and coastal areas, especially those of the National Trust, and most commons.
▪ Some woods and forests, especially those owned by the Forestry Commission.
▪ Country parks and picnic sites.
▪ Most beaches.
▪ Towpaths on canals and rivers.
▪ Some land that is being rested from agriculture, where notices allowing access are displayed.
▪ Some private paths and tracks. Consent sometimes extends to riding horses and pedal cycles.
Ask for advice if you are unsure

For your information
▪ County and metropolitan district councils and London boroughs have a duty to protect, maintain and record rights of way, and hold registers of commons and village greens - report problems you find to them.
▪ Obstructions, dangerous animals, harassment and misleading signs on rights of way are illegal.
▪ If a public path runs along the edge of a field, it must not be ploughed or disturbed.
▪ A public path across a field can be ploughed or disturbed to cultivate a crop, but the surface must be quickly restored and the line of the path made apparent on the ground.
▪ Crops (other than grass)

must not be allowed to inconvenience the use of a rights of way, or prevent the line from being apparent on the ground.
▪ Landowners can require you to leave land to which you have no right of access.
▪ Motor vehicles are normally permitted only on roads, byways and some roads used as public paths.
▪ Follow any local bylaws.

And, wherever you go, follow the Country Code.
(see page 14)

This Charter is for practical guidance in England and Wales only. Fuller advice is given in a free booklet 'Out in the Country' available from Countryside Commission Postal Sales, PO Box 124, Walgrave, Northampton NN6 9TL, telephone (01604) 781848. Published with kind permission of the Countryside Commission.